Every great jazz player knows the importance of listening to learn. Any language needs to be learned through listening in order to learn its nuances. As an improvisor develops their vocabulary he or she then must free themselves from conventional thinking and try new things. Even if what they play sounds good they still try new things, even things that they think will sound bad because some ideas may be great. This free flow thinking is what Gray McQuarrie has applied to business and life. A great improvisor knows learning never ends and only ego gets in the way of learning. Gray has clearly defined how to stay on track when it comes to business. Sounds simple but it is a "DAM" good idea.

–Tony D'Aveni,
Jazz Trumpet Player, Music Composer

My show explores how businesses become the best. I have seen many of the scenarios described in this book on our show. Gray McQuarrie offers unique insights how to dramatically improve the way you do business and life... Change your Dam Thinking is truly mind-flowing and business changing. Get your "Dam" copy today!

–Todd Dean,
Bestselling Author and Host"The Best Business Show"
WNYM AM 970 The Apple, New York City

Gray's book is a provocative and practical look at the challenges of business today. I have been working with Gray for the past three years and we have been able to make incredible advances in our business by challenging the status quo. We have learned a valuable set of lessons in that we know that work is social and the entire operation is interconnected. Gray's definition of the different "dams" that have clogged the flow of our operations have been instrumental in developing our strategies to improve everything from our internal design and development activities to our interfaces with our customers in solving their problems. I look forward to continuing our work with Gray and we take our company to new levels of growth and profitability!

–Mark B. Thomas,
CEO, HEI, Inc.

I have known Gray McQuarrie as a colleague and friend for more than two decades. We have multiple shared business successes as well as sharing a patent. I have never met a consultant who was more committed to the success of his clients than Gray. In the past few years Gray has generalized and codified his methods for identifying and solving problems. All that congealed wisdom is in the book you are holding. Enjoy!

–Dr. Bradley Jones,
Director of Research and Development for
JMP Software, A Division of SAS

Change Your DAM Thinking is a must-read. Gray McQuarrie's vast experience in Business Transformation will be of tremendous value to anyone wanting to improve bottom line profits by increasing FLOW. He points out the pitfalls and provides processes which can help both beginners and industry veterans avoid costly mistakes and develop a winning culture.

–Bill Sezate,
General Manager HEI Inc. and Lean Manufacturing Expert

Change Your

DAM

Thinking

How to Design a Company that FLOWS & GROWS

Change Your

DAM

Thinking

How to Design a Company that FLOWS & GROWS

GRAY MCQUARRIE

BOUND
PUBLISHING

Bound Publishing
A division of Dean Global Group Inc.

United States
6501 E. Greenway Pkwy
#103-480
Scottsdale, AZ
85254

Canada
Suite 114
720 28th St. NE
Calgary, AB T2A 6R3

Toll Free Phone and Fax: 1-888-237-1627
Email: info@boundpublishing.com

ISBN (softcover): 978-0-9867233-2-2
ISBN (ebook): 978-0-9867233-1-5

Cover: Lloyd Arbour
Text: Lloyd Arbour
Edit: Michelle Baer & Bound Publishing

This book is dedicated to my late grandfather,
William F. Dietrich

I continue to model after him...

CONTENTS

FOREWORD

Shipley Company

---

*Aerodynamically, the bumble bee shouldn't
be able to fly, but the bumble bee doesn't know it
so it goes on flying anyway.*

—Mary Kay Ash

*This quote hung outside the door to Charlie Shipley's
office at Shipley Company, Newton Lower Falls, Massachusetts.*

Along the Charles River in Newton Lower Falls I stood in the 2nd floor cafeteria of an oddly shaped, almost eccentric building. The building had been designed by my father Charlie Shipley. Charlie was an inventor, and dreamer. Charlie's view of the world was artistic, creative, unrestrained, and always positive. He was an entrepreneur.

He was to start a business that revolutionized the electronic chemical market. The business started on an idea, a dream. Nothing more. What made it so different, is the fact that it was a husband and wife team. My father was the creative genius, and my mother was the tough minded COO who made sure we made payroll each week. The business started in the basement of our house. I was 12 years old. I remember how upset I felt when the pool table, which I was not allowed to use but used anyway, was converted into a lab bench. In short order our neighbors justifiably complained about the increasingly large deliveries of chemicals and supplies in our residential street. So Charlie designed the building where I was currently standing. It was on old mill converted and expanded to house the corporate headquarters for our high technology business. Our business depended on speed and quality. How appropriate that the river, fast and clear, was currently raging outside the cafeteria window!

This was a company that started from nothing and grew quickly. It was the company that invented positive working photoresists—light sensitive materials used to make dense semiconductor manufacturing possible. It was the company that invented the catalyst essential for plated-through holes on printed circuit boards, which made it possible to connect these dense semiconductors into the electronic devices we know today. Globally, so many of us have touched a product that required Shipley chemistry; be it a computer, camera, cell phone or TV. It was a company that the DuPont's, Ciba Geigy's, Dow's and Rohm & Haas's lusted to acquire. Electronic chemicals were sexy, high growth, high gross margin businesses demanding the latest technology processes and equipment that supplied the highest technology companies on Earth. And I had just become the president. I did not want to screw up what my parents had so successfully launched. I knew this business could not tolerate a major mistake or strategic misstep. I was both excited and frightened about running this company. That it was a family business only added to the pressure.

So there I was. It was 9:30am and the company cafeteria was standing room only. This was my first two way, open communication, Quarterly Business Review. I knew if I was going to stay on top of this wild, but unrestrained racehorse called Shipley that I needed communication and trust at every level, at every location, by every employee. This was one forum that needed to work. I would start other types of communication forums as well as I began to understand the needs of the business, the needs of our customers, and the needs of our people. On this day, my first meeting with the troops, I not only wished to present the state of the business, but I also wanted to know what was on our employees' minds and what they were thinking. I was very much looking forward to my first Q&A session confident I could handle anything thrown my way!

So there I was in the cafeteria. Exhorting the troops onward. Reduce new product cycle time, improve quality, improve our sales, and improve our information systems among other items. You have heard it all. The Business Review was going well. Naturally, it was going well—the company was doing well. But you cannot freeze frame or "pause" the good times. Our technology was enabling. Which is another way of saying it moved lightning fast. There were huge challenges. Our fortunes could change on a dime. I was feeling very upbeat. And then came the Q&A. Earlier I had reported that a major customer, Intel, who had rated us harshly for poor quality on one of our products in the past, a situation that put this business at risk, had rated us highly on a recent review. We all felt very good about it. Patted ourselves on the back, and felt very relaxed and relieved. Then it happened... There was a voice in the rear of the cafeteria. One of "those kind" of questions followed. You know the kind. The kind that on the surface looks like a softball, but is no softball. Forces you to think.

Really think. It was Gray... "How did our major competitor score in the quality audit at this account?" Uh oh! I had neglected to ask or even think to ask that question. Obviously, our company needs to be improving at a much faster rate than our competitors. If we aren't, then who cares how our customer scored us!

Quality in the photoresist business was critical. Our manufacturing operations had to continuously raise their standards stretching our engineering and manufacturing knowhow all of the time. Quality was huge. We could not afford to shutdown our customer's multibillion dollar manufacturing operations. Almost instantly, I too wanted to know the answer to this question. And I didn't know it. I made eye contact with my executive team and a few others and I could see from their faces, they had not thought to ask this question either. In a way I was embarrassed. Because I knew we should have thought to ask that question. And in a way I hated Gray, because I had to say, "We don't know the answer, but we will get back to you." But I knew better. You cannot hate Gray! So, we went back to the customer and asked. Intel's response was simply "we were wondering when you would get around to asking us that question."

That one simple, seemingly harmless question revealed a major weakness in the company that left unchecked would have gotten me and Shipley in serious trouble. As president this question showed me and my team we could never become complacent. We could never take things for granted without asking more probing questions that get beneath the surface. We had to move fast and improve every day. Our business success depended on velocity, quality and our ability to adapt and create market disruptive products. Products that would emerge out of the collective intelligence of our people. And we had very, very smart people! Gray's question reminded me that every day was a race. We did not have time to pat each other on the back and rest on our laurels. Slowing down ever so slightly would be fatal. We had very tough global competition.

With each meeting I had developed a love/hate relationship with Gray's questions.

My awkward feelings became center stage and I was uncomfortable at not having a good answer. Questions like, "what I thought of Malcolm Baldridge?" He wanted to see if I was going to answer the man or the award! And just before I was going to answer the obvious question, I stopped myself and asked him, "Gray, do you mean the man or the award?" I began to quickly realize that the inquisitive, irreverent, bold personality and mind was what this company needed to grow fast. Gray was part of a new crop of employees that had been recently hired to support Shipley's next wave of new products and technology. They mixed well with our existing employees. We called them members, company members. We were just at the start of understanding this new fresh blood. They were leaving their imprint on this company fast and I liked it. I liked it a lot.

Shipley continued to grow fast. Not without ups and downs, and it was never easy! We were acquired by Rohm & Haas, and in time the company name was changed from Shipley Company to Rohm & Haas Electronic Materials. We had grown to a fast growing, very profitable, $1 billion business at the time of the name change. Amazing what that little business started in the basement had become!

Many people in the industry still refer to the products as Shipley products. Apparently they can't help themselves. I think that speaks volumes about the Shipley brand and what it represents. Quality product combined with quality service. Quality was culturally ingrained into our business at an early stage by my mother. "Quality of product, quality of our people, always integrity". Still, complacency is insidious. Assumptions follow—"of course our quality is good." It is too easy to believe our own press. Gray's questions were prickly. Intentionally so. He assumed nothing. His questions would always probe and force real thought. Execution is where rubber meets road. And continually improving quality throughout all operations including shortening new product development time was critical to our success.

Over the years I spent time with Gray as a friend. We both love to road bike and we have had many demanding all day bicycle trips to Flagstaff, the Ozarks, the White Mountains, and even the Southern Alps outside of Nice, France! Like business, exhilarating stuff with ups and down, twists and turns, and always unpredictable, uncontrollable environment. Not surprisingly, the warm-up always consisted of a business discussion. This was Gray's passion; how could we be better. And his favorite theme, "what makes a company great?" And I needed the help! I needed the thinking that was generated from his questions, from his discussions, and from his ideas. I came to know Gray as humorous, slightly twisted, gregarious at times, meditative at other times, but always a deep thinker. I came to learn, he enjoys getting others to think deeply too.

If you're looking for a formula driven textbook, or consulting type book, don't waste your time here. If you want to think, really think, and understand how you can fully engage an organization's capacity, this book will help. But again, no formulas, no guarantees. Life is too complex and lady luck always has a role to play. But with preparation your odds improve tremendously. I like this book!

Like the cycling, if you decide to proceed, strap on your racing gear, and get ready for a ride! At minimum you will have a lot of fun!!!

–Richard Shipley
May, 2010

PREFACE

In 1977 my grandfather, William F. Dietrich, retired as a board member of Medtronic.

Earl Bakken, the father of the first battery-operated, transistorized pacemaker, cofounder, and the first CEO of Medtronic, had this to say about my grandfather at the annual 1977 stockholders meeting:

> Bill Dietrich, who retired from our Board of Directors during the past fiscal year, joined the board in early 1962, a time in Medtronic's history when we were in serious financial difficulty. He was instrumental in helping us secure loans, providing the money we needed to keep going. But beyond this, he was a great assistance to me personally. He represented wise counsel on the board, someone with whom I could check my ideas. He was a person to learn from, particularly in his attitudes toward people and life. He understood and trusted people and knew how to develop trust and motivation. His influence on this company has been great. Much of his personal philosophy is embodied in our six basic objectives, and I want to recognize him for his contributions.

In the summer of 1994, Earl Bakken announced his retirement from the board. I wrote him a letter.

Wm. Gray McQuarrie
13025 Twin Meadows Ct.
St. Louis, MO 63146
8/4/94

Earl Bakken
Medtronic
7000 Central Avenue, NE
Minneapolis, MN 55432-3575

Dear Mr. Bakken,

I am the grandson of William F. Dietrich. My folks, Don and Lori, live in Edina, Minnesota. I'm the one in the family that got a chemical engineering degree from the University of Minnesota and has ventured out in the world. I have worked for a small computer firm in Salt Lake City, Utah, to Kollmorgen, a large electronics company on Long Island (most of my friends from there work for AMP-AKXO) to a materials company Norplex/Oak, in LaCrosse WI, which is now Allied Signal Laminates, to a specialty chemical company called Shipley, now part of Rohm and Haas, and currently I am a Senior Process Development Specialist with Monsanto in St. Louis, MO working in a small fledgling start up venture within the chemical group. In my 11 years with large and small companies I have seen a lot, and I have seen a lot that was wrong. And this is what has motivated me to write to you.

I saw from the annual report that you are retiring from the board. I am glad for you and your success, but as a stockholder, I am concerned, because I know the type of leader you were and what it meant to employees and customers alike. I remember how surprised and happy you made my Grandfather from the comments you made at the board meeting when he retired from the board. I have read those comments many times. Also I have read your mission statement many times. As a young person trying to find the truth of what makes a business grow, while another withers and disappears, I find tiny hints in these statements. I need to read these statements as well as books about Deming, etc, because as a country I think we are way off track in how we manage and run our businesses. My grandfather had a keen sense of what was right in a business, not appreciating that others did not have this same level of understanding. To him, it was all "common sense." Further, past events did not interest him. He always was looking ahead, which was one of his many strengths.

With this background, I wish to start a conversation with you, and maybe plant a seed for an idea. I think there is a real need for someone like myself to know how Medtronic came to be. What were your problems? How did you solve them? What would you have done differently? What did you learn? What should others know? In ancient cultures, stories were the fabric that kept things together. In the culture of business I don't think there are enough stories from real people that actually built a business. As a result I think mistakes are repeated over and over again. Big companies are struggling to make new businesses. They hire consultants. They expect miracles. There is impatience. And before too long the little company not only doesn't get off the ground, but the big company begins to shrink fast. As you know my grandfather wrote a book. The type of book I am asking for is different. It is the type of book my grandfather couldn't write for many reasons. I know he felt it would just be an ego thing for him and he found great distaste in that. But us younger guys need to learn your lessons. We want to hear your stories.

Regards,

Gray

Six days later, I got a letter back from Earl Bakken, written from his home in Hawaii.

Earl E. Bakken

Kiholo Bay, North Kona Coast, Island of Hawaii

August 10, 1994

Wm. Gray McQuarrie
13025 Twin Meadows Ct.
St. Louis, MO 63146

Dear Mr. McQuarrie,

Thank you for your letter dated August 4, 1994. It is true that I will "retire" from the board at the annual meeting this August 31. However, I will attend some board meetings and will continue as an active consultant to the company for as long as I am able.

Your Grandfather was a wonderful mentor to me. When he came on the board, it was the money that came with him from Community Investment Enterprises that filled Medtronics immediate need, but in the long run his wisdom and counsel was worth a thousand times the value of the money.

In regard to your thought about a book - I am currently working on one that will hopefully be completed in about a year. My input into the book is done and the writer is gathering more material from other people who participated in the earlier days. This book will give a detailed history of the company and its people, and hopefully how we succeded.

I am sending a couple of things that may be of value to you 1. Refelections on Leadership that I wrote and 2. a book called New Traditions in Business has a message that I am sure your Grandfather would have approved.

If you ever have a chance to get to the Big Island of Hawaii, please, I would like to invite you to our home for lunch. I am enclosing my card with my address and telephone number on it for your future reference.

My best wishes to you for a successful career. Model after your Grandfather and success is assured.

With Aloha,

Earl E. Bakken

Between fiscal 1962 and 1968, sales rose from $518,000 to $10 million. Net income leaped from nonexistent to a million dollars during the same period. Our "little family," meanwhile, grew almost tenfold—from fewer than 40 employees to nearly 350.

—Earl Bakken
One Man's Full Life, 1999

Today, Medtronic is a $15 billion company with an EBITDA of over $5 billion.

ACKNOWLEDGMENTS

I have to thank my mother and my late father, who created within me the desire to be successful and passionate about my life. If my dad were alive today I know he would be very proud of me for writing this book. He loved writing, literature, and books. He knew I was good at math but I struggled with writing and reading as a child. He would spend many hours with me as I read to him. My mom would spend many hours a week showing flash cards to me prior to my spelling tests. Without their dedicated efforts as loving parents this book would not have been written.

I have to acknowledge my brother in law, Phil Colton, who helped me find my first "ideal" client and introduced me to Mark Thomas. Working with Mark Thomas and HEI helped to distill my thinking. I also thank Mark for the many discussions we had that helped with this book. I have to acknowledge Bill Brandell for forcing me to think deeper and to simplify and consolidate my ideas so that I would come up with something, not just interesting, but useful. Many of the ideas in this book not only originate from my decades of work in industry, but from the many years of discussions I have had with Dr. Frank Delk.

I would also like to thank many of the people who encouraged me and worked with me as I wrote this book: Bill Sezate, Chuck Russo, Dave Moldenhaur, Bradley Jones, Rich Pangier, Julia Mulligan, Dee Burks who did a fantastic job coaching me through the writing process, Richard Shipley, Tony D'Aveni, Kim Klien, Gerry Klien, Michelle Baer, and last but not least, Gina Hayden.

Finally I have to thank Terry Whiting who beat down my ego dam and reinforced in me the importance of listening and observing.

ABOUT THE BOOK

Each chapter in this book consists of stories. There is a moral to these stories: you will grow as a flow thinker and you will be damned as a dam thinker. The choice is yours.

In order to design your company so that it flows and grows, I have given you complex solutions described at the end of each chapter: the story points. After you read this book, you may want to try out some of these story points. I encourage you to do that— to experiment and learn, to improvise and create, to discover and make better. When you see the world as a flow thinker, you will find all sorts of complex solutions that you can collect and try out as you see fit. This is a book that will make you the designer, the innovator, the creator of your own business system; you won't learn someone else's system and paint by numbers! You are the designer for your company. You may already see the paint splatter on your shirt, tie and shoes.

In Chapter 10 you will see an outline of how to design and cast your own complex plan from a backlog of complex solutions. You can't flow and grow without a complex plan. A complex plan exploits dependencies. A complex plan means that a number of things happen at the same time in parallel. A complex plan focuses on action and requires adaptation and improvisation. A complex plan exploits the fact that work is social, that our behaviors will lead results, and that our behaviors are governed by our thinking. In order to change our work result, we must change our dam-thinking to flow-thinking.

Changing to flow-thinking and making teamwork social was exactly Herb Brook's message to the United States Olympic Hockey Coach Selection Committee in 1979. Herb presented them with a complex plan. They chose him, and the rest is history.

INTRODUCTION

Being the Best in the World

The legs feed the wolf!

—Herb Brooks

I was born and raised in a very cold state—Minnesota. Everyone played hockey. I wasn't a hockey player, but on rare occasion I would lace up my skates and play a little. When I was in high school, everyone knew who Herb Brooks was. I remember once going to Williams Arena on the University of Minnesota campus, sitting under the old, cold rafters, and watching the Golden Gophers destroy the University of Minnesota–Duluth. I had never seen anything like it. Everything moved so fast. It would start at the far end of the ice behind their own net, and then it would flow in smooth, fast lines and curves, ending with the puck in the Duluth net. It was extremely difficult to comprehend what was going on—who was a forward, who was a defenseman, who was supposed to play on the right, and who was supposed to play on the left. It looked uncontrolled, loose, and improvised. But it wasn't undisciplined. Herb's team flowed. There was velocity, quality, and emergence. Sure, the Gophers were good that night, but not good enough to beat a professional team like the North Stars or, for that matter, the best hockey team in the world, the Russian hockey team. Herb chose a completely different path to train and motivate the 1980 Olympic USA hockey team. Why?

The scale was different. The European rink was a different size—significantly wider. In a game such as hockey, if you change the dimensions just a little bit, then how best to play the game changes too. Anytime you are dealing with a complex system such as a hockey game or the complex interactions within your company, how best to run it is highly dependent on scale. You will see the importance scale has to any business in Chapter 6: Scale-Up Insanity.

The objective was different. He wanted to beat the best hockey team in the world with a bunch of college kids. It was an impossible fantasy. There was no element of reality contained in it. But just the thought of what it would feel like to accomplish it was too compelling, too motivating, just too gosh-darn-inspiring. In Chapter 2: The Four Business States, you will see that without an ambitious, impossible goal, your company will not have any drive. You will also see in Chapter 2 that if you don't have a flow-thinking culture in your company, your dream will never come true. The 1980 USA hockey team was all about flow, and they had an ambitious, impossible goal.

The amount of time to create a team was ambitious—there was little time to prepare. In less than a year, kids who hardly knew each other would have to be so unified as a team that they would think of themselves, and behave together, as a true family. Without a complex, ingrained, family behavior, Team USA stood no chance. Their work of winning would be highly social, flowing, and extremely powerful.

Work is social! Herb took the social point of view of his team probably farther than any coach in any sport. The *work is social* theme appears throughout this entire book.

What Herb proposed was very different—it had never been seen before in U.S. hockey. The selection committee had a choice. They could go with the traditional approach, but they knew the outcome: failure and disaster for U.S. hockey. There was another choice—a style of play where the team would flow and improvise and create on the ice in a highly dependent way, forcing the opposing team to be entirely reactive. Improvising is powerful. Few companies preach it. In fact, what they preach is control—dam control! Chapter 9: The Art of Improvising will reveal the secrets to improvising so you can do it too.

What Herb created in order to beat the Russians was a simple, yet complex plan. They wouldn't let the Russians set the pace of the game; *they* would set the pace of the game. The Russians wouldn't control the puck; *they* would control the puck. Team USA would beat the Russians at their own game. The only way this could happen was by having a team that was better conditioned than the Russians.

The legs feed the wolf! This mantra explains why it was a complex plan. Everything depended on conditioning. Remove the conditioning, remove the legs, and all else is meaningless. There would be no food. There would be no medal.

A complex plan can be simple if you focus on only a few ideas at one time and drive them relentlessly. What makes it complex is that these few ideas improve a whole host of other things all at once. So few business managers today see the world as a complex, organic, connected thing. Herb understood the few advantages he had, such as young legs that could be made as strong as steel. He also had young minds that were malleable and could learn new ideas quickly. Chapter 7: The Very Best Plans Never Survive the First Bullet and Chapter 10: Creating Your Own Complex Plan will show you how to develop your own simple, yet complex plans.

Herb also understood the art of improvising, which is discussed in Chapter 9. Improvising is about creating in real time. It requires practice and discipline in order to be able to do it. Often, when we see something improvised, we think it is undisciplined. It isn't. Herb had the team think about and master only a few ideas. Then, he had them combine these ideas in different permutations. The number of patterns that the team could create on the ice and productively use to wear down a team and score was close to infinite. Complexity, improvising, and creativity work very well together under a flow paradigm. It will make your company extremely competitive.

To get his players to think in terms of flow, Herb had to break down all of the dam-thinking in his players' heads. We talk about these dams in Chapter 5: The Five Thinking Dams and How They Stop Flow. One of the worst thinking dams to have on any team or company is the *feelings* dam. It is the most challenging dam for people to deal with and get rid of. What Herb did was genius. He made it clear to the team that he wasn't their friend. He wasn't going to be part of their family. Instead he was going to be the *prod*. The force to be reckoned with. The force that always reminded them of their purpose. The force that would permanently etch into their brains the few ideas that would create a complex flow. Herb was the force that would unite these individuals as a team as they tried to overcome the challenges he constantly put in front of them.

What Herb did by staying at arm's length from the social connection and human affections of the team is difficult for many of us to understand. This isn't what Herb did at the University of Minnesota; but, again, he knew he had to get everything he could out of these kids. If he got too close, he would start to get wrapped up in their feelings and back off from what he was trying to make them do. As you will see in Chapter 5, as well as in many other sections of the book, the more you get wrapped up in people's feelings, the more you lose focus with the ultimate objective. Herb knew he had to stay focused on the ultimate objective. He could not let his feelings or the feelings of his team get in the way.

Herb held the team to high standards. Think of a standard as a constraint: minimally acceptable performance. A famous quote from Herb Brooks is, "If you give me 99 percent you will make my job very easy." Accountability is a very powerful tool that business leaders can use, but seldom do. The most common reason is the feelings dam: a desire not to make a person feel bad or to make the business leader feel like they are a bad person. If you are going to hold your people accountable, then you must remove the feelings dam. Herb had to have emotional separation with his players. There was just no other way. In Chapter 4: What Causes People to Hate Their Job, the value of accountability is stressed. Without accountability you won't have good performance from your people and they will be unhappy. With it, your people may complain, but you will get excellent performance. And, in the end, they will be very happy and loyal to you and your company.

In chapter 8, the importance of listening and observing is stressed. Herb learned a lot by observing the Russian Hockey team and listening to the Russian coaches. If he got the chance, he would sneak in while the Russians practiced and ask the Russian coach all sorts of questions. But there is a fact that is not as appreciated as it should be: the Russian coach told Herb everything that he wanted to know. If you ask, you will be surprised at how much information and help is at your fingertips. In Chapter 5, the *ego* dam and the *learning* dam are presented. The ego dam occurs when we don't ask for help but we should. The learning dam occurs when we think we know everything; hence, we fail to discover anything new, and that prevents us from growing. Often, dams feed off of one another. For example, if your ego makes you think you know everything, then you are never going to ask for help. You might find this problem with a two year old, a teenager or a bad manager. Herb was not afflicted with any thinking dams, which is rare for anyone.

The greatest point hardly ever made about the 1980 USA hockey team experience was that the feat was never repeated! Why? The answer to this question reveals my entire motivation for this book. Herb's thinking was completely different. It was all about flow. I call Herb's brand of seeing and thinking about the world flow-thinking. The opposite choice for seeing and thinking about the world is dam-thinking. Right now, at this moment, you have a choice: to be a flow thinker or a dam thinker. In order to understand what Herb did, and to get a result like Herb got, you have to be a flow thinker. In order to do that, you have to give up your dam-thinking. You can't have both. Flow-thinking and dam-thinking are the opposite of each other; they are mutually exclusive. The problem is that we are all trained to be dam thinkers. This book is an attempt to lead and motivate you to make the right choice. Only a flow thinker can design a company that flows and grows and achieves unlimited growth.

Any company can become great, but few do. The first place I learned this rule was at my first professional engineering job at Beehive Circuits, in Salt Lake City, Utah.

STORY POINT 1:
Build Trust by Setting High Performance Standards

Herb set the standard right out of the gate, "If you give me 99 percent, you will make my job very easy." The standards he set created communication and trust. Why is that important to you?

When communication is blocked because of a trust dam you won't get the information you need. You will likely be the last to know of a disaster. You will be constantly surprised. You will be under a high level of stress.

Herb had trust dams among his players. They had competed against each other, and there were deep feelings of resentment, envy, and blame. Everyone had baggage. In the movie Miracle, which depicts the growth and evolution of the team, two rival hockey players fight on the ice. You see a direct approach applied: "Tell me who you are, where you are from, and who you play for?" This tactic doesn't work. People are stubborn. In the spider web diagram below we see the spider pulling from the center. This provides maximum mechanical advantage. If the spider was close to the edge of the dam and tried to pull, the force would be very weak. The diagram suggests an indirect solution, or what I call a complex solution, will work best when you encounter a trust dam. Herb's indirect solution, was setting an individual's performance standard.

When Herb said, "Give me 99 percent and you will make my job easy," he was telling his players that they had a big part to play in his decision. They needed to figure out the effort he wanted, and they quickly learned what it was. The trust dam began to fall when Herb made it clear that they needed to be a unit, a line, and not a bunch of individuals. They had to work together. If they made the decision not to trust their teammates and not communicate the way they needed to, they would be gone. Everyone knew Herb was evaluating them all the time. Everyone knew he didn't have a single favorite player. His high standard and his social distance from the team created trust, fast. Herb executed a great, complex solution to the trust dam that you can experiment with and learn from.

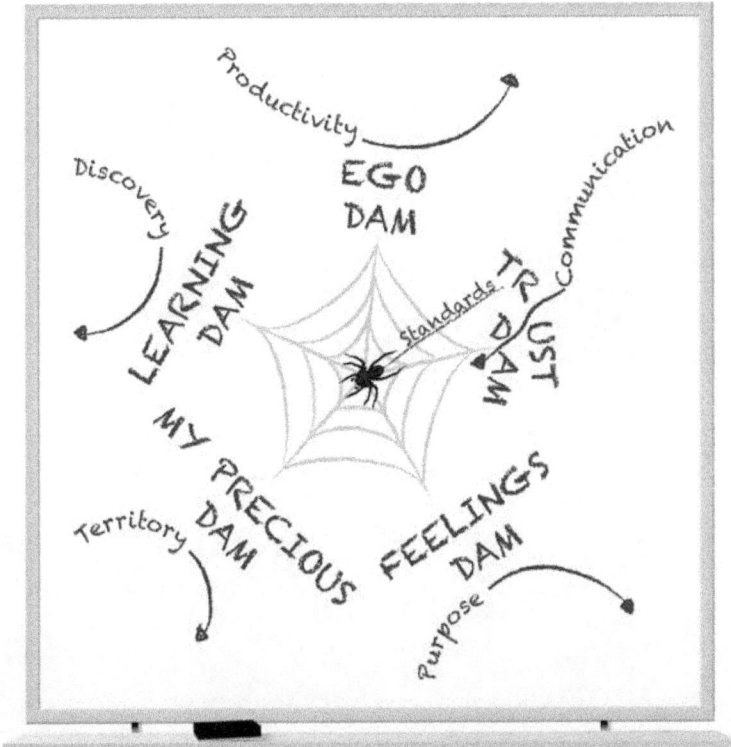

Figure 1: "Standards" Spider Diagram

The spider diagram above shows how all of the dams are connected together. When the spider is at the center of the web, it generates maximum force on all of the other dams. A good way to think of this is as a rope tied to the top of the dam, which will provide maximum mechanical advantage when you pull on it. That means the most powerful way to deal with a trust problem is indirectly. When you do that you pull on all of the other dams too! When Herb gave everyone a standard the team had to figure out for itself what needed to be done. The team members had to communicate more (trust dam), ask for help from each other (ego dam), and be open to learn (learning dam). Having all these things happen at once, just by implementing one simple thing, is why setting standards is a complex solution. The web helps us to visualize the very real interconnectedness of all of the dams and how this forced the individual team members to radically change their thinking. This in turn changed everyone's behavior so that a very powerful team could be molded by Herb. Complex solutions have been around a long time, but we are still taught to approach things with a very inefficient, linear, one-at-a-time strategy.

CHAPTER 1

My Beehive Days

---

*What you do speaks so loud that I cannot
hear what you say.*

—Ralph Waldo Emerson

What was wrong with Beehive? It was the early 1980's and Beehive was a respectable original equipment manufacturer (OEM) of computer terminals used by Digital Equipment and other companies. They had made a big bet that they could make a personal computer similar to Apple's. They anticipated that the new market for PCs would be huge, and they had constructed their business plan on the premise of capturing a very small, but very distinct, percentage of this market. This seemed like a good bet, because success would only require a small number of customers. Beehive thought they only needed to worry about making a product work. Management reasoned that making a product work would be realistic and doable. Beehive leadership and the board agreed with management and bought into the plan. Everyone could imagine success. Hardly anything would need to change. The plan was simple, easy, and realistic. The check was already in the mail! It was utter foolishness to think Beehive could be as big as Apple or IBM.

To be big you would have to start big. You would need thousands of employees. You would need enormous facilities with the latest technology and shiny, new equipment. Build it and they will come. It would be like a huge dam, with all the resources built up behind it, ready to release new products into the world. What could be generated from a small, steady stream of products from a small company? The small, steady stream of products would still produce a good business if the potential market was large enough. Beehive didn't have big money. Small was their only choice. But how small? If Beehive's plan was too ambitious, the costs would be too high. The cost would be more uncertainty, more stress, more confusion, more risk. There would be conflicts and struggles with the ambitious plan. The outcomes would be unpredictable. The golden rule—consensus—would be lost.

So many business books and business ideas, including some of the best, preach the goodness of consensus. Consensus management? Google it today and you will get hit after hit. Bottom-line consensus management is about reaching universal agreement and then, somehow, achieving commitment. It is about a deterministic world with a predictable outcome. It is about comfort. This need for everyone feeling comfortable defines the dreadful feelings dam. With a feelings dam we lose our purpose and our business becomes meaningless. And as with any dam, nothing changes; things stand still.

Consensus is about being in the middle. It is about compromise. It is the language of "buts" and "what ifs" and "playing it safe." It is the avoidance of commitment and accountability. It is about always being nice. Consensus is about people being agreeable and polite. A cause is about people uniting under a banner of purpose! A cause lives at the extreme. A cause is the language of action. The language of doing. It is the language of never giving up or settling for less. At times a cause is the language of war. *No taxation without representation! Don't tread on me!* Was the United States formed from consensus or through war? In business we must all be civil. We must all agree. We must have consensus. Or so consensus management experts say. Beehive was about consensus. Everyone was comfortable. Everything appeared perfect if you listened to the conversations. For me something didn't feel right. Was Beehive in trouble?

I was told not to worry. Occasionally, long-time employees would pull me, the newbie, aside and start to talk in a very purposeful way, explaining the genius of the plan. They would have me do the math of taking a very small percentage and multiplying it by a very large number. I got the math, but I heard a voice: what would make a customer choose us over another company? How many other companies had the exact same plan? Isn't a small percentage very close to zero? There was some talk I overheard about technological advances. Would customers want what we were offering? None of these questions mattered. The plan was all that mattered, and it had been launched.

Beehive had been the darling of Utah, from a small startup with only a few people, to a business of some 400 employees located in Salt Lake City. Everyone there—including my dad's friend, Warren Clifford, the CEO, Joe Carbone, the COO who interviewed me over the phone and hired me, and my boss Bill Rowsell, the engineering manager for the company's small printed circuit board shop, Beehive Circuits—was a good person who knew his or her job. When I watched these people, I wondered if they were happy. Often, when I was alone with my dad (who was a physician) while he was driving the car, he would say, "Son, I am really puzzled as to why people get so unhappy in business." I knew he was talking about Beehive. I wondered why working for a company would make a person unhappy. I wondered why my dad framed the question as if the answer was indefinable and mysterious?

Beehive wasn't big, but it was in a professional business park location, with professional-looking employees. By contrast, the smaller sister company, Beehive Circuits, where I worked, was a hole-in-the-wall place right next door to a Toro repair center. Nothing was fancy. The equipment was old. The operation was very modest with just a few dozen ragged-looking employees— good, hard-working people who welcomed me and taught me a great lesson. To this day I am proud to have known them. When the intercom rang, "The truck is here! The truck is here!" I went out, got my sandwich, and sat down with them. After awhile I began to realize that each of them, in some corner of his or her mind, wanted to be a part of something important, something significant, something they could be proud of—if they only were asked.

Making printed circuit boards is messy. My clothes would have holes. My white lab coat would have blue, green, and orange blotches after only a week. Messy and modest as it was, this was the start to my career—a long, rewarding, interesting, and stimulating career in making companies better. Because Beehive Circuits was so small, I saw an entire business operate: procurement, operations, engineering, technology, human resources, sales, and sales engineering. Almost every day there were new surprises. Someone from MacDermid, a highly respected plating chemistry supplier, might step into my office (which was a desk in the corner of a small reception lobby area) and teach me about recent industry advances. A manufacturing representative who had spent many years working at Control Data might spend a day helping me on the production floor with my plating problems. Then there was the immediate disaster at the Beehive mother company up the road in their assembly operation. The finger of blame would descend on us, the motley crew of Beehive Circuits, and an immediate, drop everything response was demanded.

I learned that if I were just willing to ask for help, there was a world of resources available to tap into. It started with the suppliers. I learned that if you treated your suppliers well, your suppliers would back you, get you out of trouble, and teach you. I saw early on that how a company treated its suppliers would often determine a company's fate. You can read a company's culture by watching how a company treats its suppliers. I began to read people's faces and study their attitudes and behaviors to determine whether things were okay at Beehive. I did this by instinct. A primitive instinct. Even though I liked my job, something didn't feel right, and I picked up on that partly from the suppliers. The suppliers sort of had a numb attitude that lacked excitement. When they came to Beehive from a big company up the road, it was as if they could let their hair down and relax. There was no urgency. There was just comfort. I felt there was a dark cloud on the horizon. Something was wrong and I couldn't put my finger on it.

What was wrong with Beehive? Things weren't going as planned. I recall standing out back, near some drums, some scrap metal, and a wire fence, looking up at the Wasatch Mountains with the sure knowledge that I had to leave Beehive fast. It was 1983 and the snowfall had been very heavy. It was a once-in-a-lifetime snow pack for skiers that year. I didn't know all of that snow was about to create a major problem that would almost destroy the Glen Canyon Dam. If the dam failed it would create a catastrophe. I had no idea that the snow I was looking at was creating a problem that correlated directly to what was wrong with Beehive.

After World War II, someone had a genius idea to put a dam at Glen Canyon: a big dam that would flood the entire canyon and create Lake Powell. For all sorts of reasons, nobody questioned the dam. In fact, the dam was built via a consensus between the Sierra Club and the U.S. Bureau of Reclamation. Everyone was comfortable with the dam size and dam location. Everyone was happy with the dam plan. Construction started in 1956 with the hope that the creation of the dam would generate a lively surrounding economy—a dam economy. If you build the dam, people will come! It took decades for the water to collect behind the dam. But with the 1983 snowfall, reality was about to hit the dam hard. The water in the mountains nearly took out the dam.

But was the idea of the dam a good one? When reality crashes into a plan achieved from consensus, you get regret, as was the case for David Brower, the executive director of the Sierra Club at that time. In the book, *The Place No One Knew*, edited by Brower, he states...

Glen Canyon died, and I was partly responsible for its needless death. Neither you nor I, nor anyone else, knew it well enough to insist that at all costs it should endure. When we began to find out, it was too late.

Reality was about to descend on Beehive. And it was too late. Beehive had a dam plan in a dam culture, and it was about to experience a serious dam problem.

So there I was, at Beehive Circuits, standing in my white lab coat, with my pipette in one hand and beaker in the other, my jeans splattered with chemistry-related holes, my tennis shoes tattered, needing a haircut, and looking up at those mountains. What was the problem? I thought that if I did a good job, figured out how to control the processes better, and improved all of the technical issues in my purview, I could make a positive impact. After all, I was highly skilled and had shown my employer how dedicated I was and how fast I could learn. I wanted to be the best employee I could possibly be and show them that they didn't make a mistake. Joe Carbone had originally called me some months prior to tell me they didn't want me. I heard what he said, but I wasn't buying what he was selling. After so many rejections, during a time when so many chemical engineers were being fired because of the recent oil glut, I was determined to be hired. I just wouldn't accept anything else. I was like the little girl Napoleon Hill talks about in *Think and Grow Rich*: I wanted my 50 cents and I wasn't going to take no for an answer. Joe abruptly changed his mind and hired me right then and there over the phone. After I was hired, I worked very hard and kept that same determined attitude, but nothing I knew or did seemed to make any difference. I was discouraged and worried.

I really wanted to show everyone I was going to do everything in my power to do the best job I possibly could. I didn't realize that by doing those things in the environment of Beehive at that time, I was potentially damaging myself and my boss. I had gone out and purchased an IBM PC with two floppy drives and 256K in internal memory, which I used to generate graphs of the production line data and quality information with Lotus 1-2-3, which I then printed out on my ten-pound dot matrix printer. Bill presented these charts one day at the weekly production review meeting and immediately Joe Carbone asked, "Where did those slides come from!" When Bill told him they were produced on an IBM PC using a dot matrix printer recently purchased by his engineer, no one said a word for the rest of the meeting. Everyone was in deep thought. Apparently, none of them had understood how far personal computer capabilities had advanced in such a short period of time. They were all quiet because they were all trying to make a personal decision: face the reality that the window was closing fast or pretend that it wasn't happening and everything was OK.

A couple of months later, I was sending my résumé out and getting interviews at places such as Photocircuits in Glen Cove, Long Island, New York. My dad thought I was crazy and wanted to talk to me about my impending defection after the Beehive board meeting. He flew down from Minneapolis and after attending the board meeting, met me for dinner at the top of the old Hotel Utah, right across the street from the Mormon Tabernacle. As we ate, I noticed his eyes looked right through me. He wasn't talking at all. He quietly said, "Son, it might be smart for you to accept that job in New York." Wow! I knew that something had gone very wrong and there was no fixing it.

I received the first clue that things were going off course some months earlier when the head of quality for Beehive asked the question, "What is quality?" The problem was that everyone had a different answer. The answers weren't just a little bit different, but widely varied and were even contradictory. Nobody had a clue. Suspense was in the air. I waited. The quality manager spoke. With an attitude of superiority and dominance over the poor, confused souls spread out in front of him, he proclaimed for all to hear, accept, and follow that "Quality is nothing more than meeting customer specifications!" My mouth hung open. I was astonished. This was a directive—a law. A bad law. It demanded obedience. No debate. No question. No conversation. Everyone was deflated. They were hoping to be inspired. They wanted to be moved to be better.

This quality directive had no passion and passion inspires people. There was discord. Personal standards and the search for meaning crashed against this ho-hum quality definition. Do you try to pull the company up by yourself? Do you step down and lower your own standards? Or, do you just leave and do something else? That feeling of discord, which the quality manager failed to see, caused the dreadful side effects to start brewing—and those side effects caused unhappiness. Standing there, looking up at the mountains, I wondered why the quality manager hadn't asked the rugged crew of Beehive Circuits what they needed to be great?

I had an inkling something was wrong when I met the mysterious plant manager who talked to me the first day, sitting some 15 feet away from me while my chair was pinned against the opposite wall. He sat behind his desk, talking in a whisper of a voice that I couldn't understand. I rarely ever saw him and never saw him on the factory floor. I don't think he liked people. He certainly wasn't interested in me. And he was never around. My boss was scared of him because he was known for setting people up to fail. He would mislead, confuse, start rumors, and backstab. Why would this kind of person be in such a vital position? Why would the company permit or ignore such bad behavior?

I also sensed the frustration growing in my boss when he would storm out of his office, walk around, pace with great agitation, and say to me, "Gray, there is something you need to know. You have engineering talent. But nothing is more important than the people out there in that shop who are building product. And Gray, I know how to motivate people. I know how to get those people going. You learn how to do that and you are really going to be valuable to any company you want to work for." I would later come to know that Bill Rowsell was one of the very best bosses I would ever have.

Beehive thought they could deliver their new, not-yet-fully functioning-as-planned, PC-like product to a relatively large customer. The product was supposed to be completed in design and performance by a certain date, but the development costs grew and the delays piled up. The entire development project was all dammed up. Be that as it may, Beehive built the product hardware anyway assuming all would go well with the software and the customer would buy. I don't know if it was the delays or the product performance, but the customer decided not to buy. All the cash had been sucked out of the company and into the product sitting in finished goods. Beehive was in a state of disaster. The roots of this disaster were formed right from the start, with the uninspiring, modest plan derived from a realistic and seemingly achievable goal.

Beehive had set their sights low. And, by setting their sights low, they set everything low. They set the standards for their people low. They set the performance of the product low. They set the quality for the products low. If we set our goal low, wouldn't that increase our chance of being successful? After all, what if we fail, because we set the goal too high? Wouldn't we feel bad? Wouldn't that ruin us? That conversation pushes us to go for the bottom-feeding goal—a goal that ensures failure. What we think is what we become. We need an ambitious goal. We need to set our sights high—so high, in fact, that we can't see how to get there—but so exciting to think about. It is so exciting that we can't help thinking about it all of the time! And before you know it, we don't know how, we do it! If you watch the movie *The Secret,* near the start there is a talk about the power your thoughts have to attract things in your life—they call it the law of attraction.

My grandfather learned about the big goal, the power of the human mind, and the law of attraction in his early years at Green Giant under his boss Ward Cossgrove. He got Earl Bakken to aim high and to think and dream about what the company would be like, not just 5 years out, or 10 years out, or 50 years out, but 100 years out! Medtronic aimed high. Beehive aimed low. Beehive and Medtronic both achieved 400 employee status. Because of the very different way both companies saw their future, the results of the two very similar companies were dramatically different.

When I left for New York I had a mission. I wanted to learn what made a company great. I wanted to participate—even in the smallest of ways—in the process of turning a flawed company into a great company. I went out with a mind motivated to learn the great secret, because there seemed to be no in-between: a company was either great or fighting for its life. Through my journey I came to learn that the product doesn't define a company. The people producing that product and the people selling and servicing the product define a company. The first thing I say to any potential client is, "Work is social." The second thing I say is, "People's behaviors will lead business results." The third thing I say is, "People's behavior is governed by their thinking." Companies that understand these three statements don't just perform well, they completely dominate the markets they serve. The place to start with any company transformation is to change people's thinking. Anything less is just an entertaining diversion on the road of life.

STORY POINT 2:
Behaviors Lead Business Results

There is a huge difference between evaluating your people and an annual performance review. In a performance review, you always try to make a person feel good. Despite your best efforts to manage their feelings, they leave uninspired and disillusioned. That is because reviews must be fair to everyone, which means almost everyone gets the same rating or grade. Performance reviews remind us of school marking reports and the pain of being judged. At other times, it reminds us of the disillusionment that occurs when an extraordinary effort is diluted in order to produce a fair average. Nobody is inspired about being average or being just above average.

In an evaluation, you try to determine if individuals are right for your company and, if so, what they need to do to be better. It is personal. It is about how they can become great and exceed their wildest expectations. But it is also more than that. It is about how they can align themselves with the mission of your company to do good things and provide valuable products and services that make a difference in people's lives and to be rewarded financially for that good work. It's about them challenging your thinking and your company because they want (as much as you do) to work for a great company. It's about everyone being part of a connected web where everyone depends upon each other. You have to evaluate people whenever the moment is called for—not on a timetable. Evaluations aren't meant to grade—they are meant to stimulate growth and motivate the change you need to realize growth. By making your people's growth potential unlimited, you make your company's growth potential unlimited.

The quality of your people doesn't matter in a dam-thinking company. In dam-thinking, you need employees that conform to the fact that nothing is moving. You don't want to do an evaluation because you will likely inspire your employees to leave and go somewhere else. This is due to the conflict between what you say and how the company performs. I see this disconnect all the time in many companies, and as soon as I see it I know the company has a dam-thinking culture. Bottom line: not too many things matter in a dam-thinking company because not much is moving.

If you don't want to have high employee turnover and a lack of movement, and if you want to be a company where everything flows fast, you have to think differently. For example, you might think evaluations are an option. They are not. Everything matters in a flow company. The quality of the equipment, the quality of the materials, the quality of your people, and the quality of their decisions matter. Your people's skills, behaviors, and attitudes matter. If you aren't measuring that, then you will be blindsided and experience a disaster. You need evaluations because behaviors lead business results. If you don't control the quality of what is going into your flow, you will have garbage. You will have to stop the flow, put up a dam, and figure out how to feed your customers the good stuff from a vast, polluted reservoir. And if that sounds like an expensive thing to do, it is.

One of my client's employees performed a vital function for the company. Nevertheless, her bad behavior, her inability to ask for help, her complete lack of accountability, and her tendency to always blame others for poor performance created a huge crisis. After the crisis, an evaluation was done on her based on the eleven parameters shown on the following radar chart titled "Employee Y" below. This person wasn't salvageable, and everyone agreed she needed to be fired. The crisis could have been averted if the person had been evaluated throughout her work history.

Employee Y

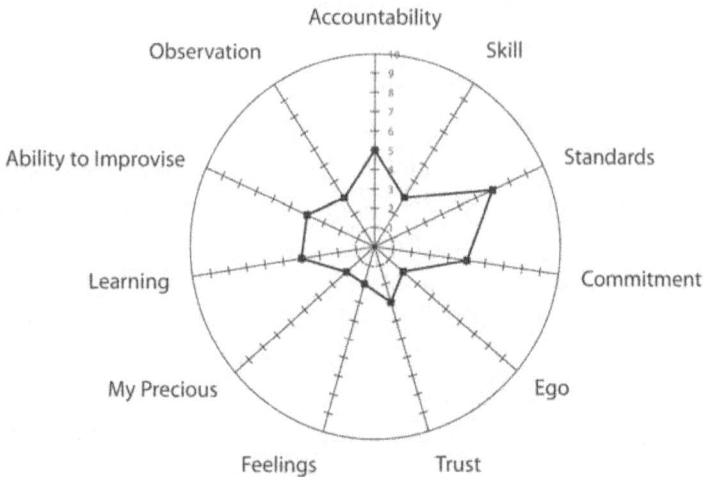

Figure 2: Evaluation Radar Chart

For each parameter in the radar chart above, 10 is good and 1 is bad. The closer the points are to the center, the worse the employee is performing. This chart contrasts an employee's skill with his or her behaviors. The behaviors are the thinking dams such as ego, trust, feelings, My Precious, learning, accountability, and commitment. The skills are improvising, observation, technical skill to do the job, and standards. This rating was for a high-level manager. If this evaluation was conducted prior to the crisis, it would have likely been averted. Note: there is nothing on here about results! Even though an employee is being rated, you can use this same radar to evaluate teams, entire factories, business units, and companies. In fact, I could see a hedge fund being created in which they evaluate the behaviors of companies to decide whether to buy or sell a stock! The reason why you can go from individual to company with an evaluation such as this is because of something called self-similarity, which is a characteristic of complex systems.

It's hard for me to think of a single instance in which a business had a disaster that wasn't related to people's bad behaviors: Tyco, Enron, WorldCom, Arthur Anderson, AIG. All of these crises could have been prevented if the executive leadership and the middle management, the people making the decisions, were evaluated. From the spider chart that follows, I indicate that the first dam to fall when you implement simple, direct, honest evaluations is the feelings dam. Evaluations should be absolutely aligned with your business purpose and not just be something that justifies some sort of privilege or entitlement. This includes the executive team— even the CEO! The CEO needs to be honestly evaluated frequently by the board of directors or by a development coach assigned to the CEO. A dam-thinking CEO is a nightmare for any company and its stock holders.

Am I making this up, or are evaluations really critical to turning a company around and changing a company's culture? IBM was turned around in the 1990's by Louis V. Gerstner. In his book, *Who Says Elephants Can't Dance?*, he describes what he did to change the slow dam-thinking culture of IBM into a higher velocity, flow-thinking culture. He says, "After a couple of years I realized that the cultural transformation was stalling… People believed in the new IBM, but they were measured and compensated—and continued to work—as if they were still in the old IBM." (210) He continues, "I needed to take the new principles … and bake them into what people did every day. And since people don't do what you expect but what you inspect, I needed to create a way to measure results." (210) If simple evaluations done frequently can change the culture of the U.S. hockey team in several weeks and a company the size of IBM within a very short period of time, what can they do for your company?

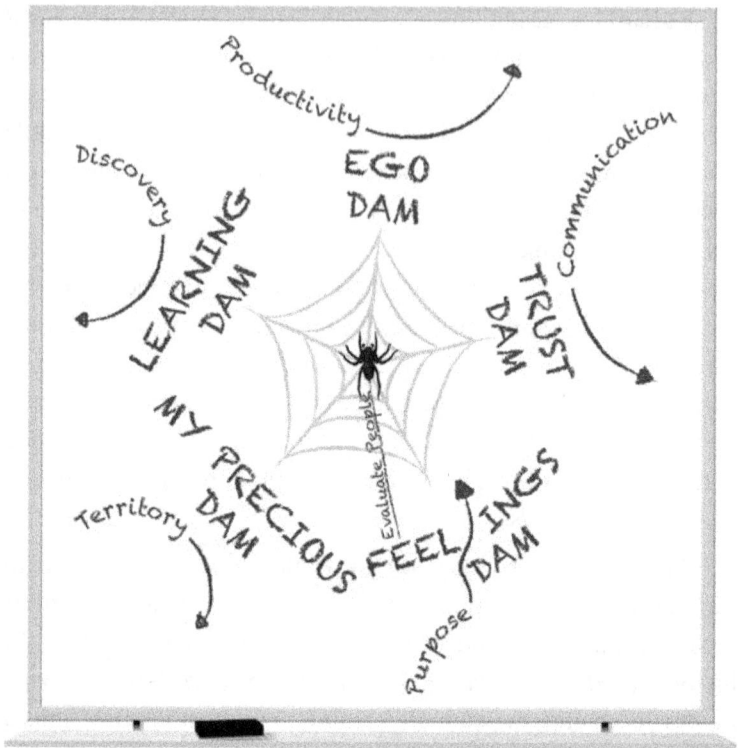

Figure 3: "Evaluate People" Spider Diagram

The spider diagram above shows how evaluating people breaks a feelings dam. You can manage the purpose of your company, or you can manage people's feelings. You can't do both. What is fair about an evaluation is that everyone is rated using the same criteria. A feelings dam is active if a manager avoids making a decision and taking action on something vitally important, because he or she is blocked by an employee's feelings, or his or her own feelings, or both. Managers who allow feelings to manipulate their decisions would be caught in an evaluation. The data for any evaluation represents good, solid observations of workplace performance and behaviors. When you see something you don't like, it is time to evaluate the person associated with that negative thing. Repetition is a very powerful learning mechanism that helps people change their thinking. Frequent evaluations are good and necessary in a flow company. The evaluations don't need to be complicated, and they don't need to take a lot of time. It takes me less than two hours to do an initial evaluation of an entire company.

CHAPTER 2

The Four Business States

Imagination is the one weapon in the
war against reality.

—Jules de Gaultier

The table that follows shows the four possible states of your business: disaster, dysfunction, goal seeking, and unlimited growth. The two columns represent the two paradigms. You choose which paradigm you want. Each paradigm will influence what you see, what you understand, and how you make decisions. The rows represent how you see the world around you. You have a choice here as well: you can use your mind merely to process the real world and make decisions strictly on facts, or you can fantasize and imagine a different world for yourself and temporarily dissociate yourself from reality. The best choice is to choose the flow-thinking paradigm and go back and forth between reality and fantasy as required.

Table 1: The Four Business States

	Paradigm	
	Dam Thinking	Flow Thinking
Reality	Dysfunction	Unlimited Growth
Fantasy	Disaster	Goal Seeking

You can travel through these states rapidly—from disaster to unlimited growth—by implementing a complex plan. For example, your plan might be to evaluate your people and hold them accountable to high standards, including specific behaviors. You can go the other way too—from unlimited growth to disaster. For example, in an attempt to profit from a rise in your company's stock price you focus your company solely on short term financial results. Through your decisions and actions you send the message that you don't care how your people think and behave. You don't care about how the results are achieved! You don't even care if what your employees do is unethical or criminal! You just want results period! When the disaster strikes, you may claim you weren't accountable, because you didn't know what your people were doing! But that would be a lie, because behaviors always lead results. It was bad behaviors that created the messes at Tyco, Enron, and Sunbeam; behaviors nurtured by the business environment the CEO created.

When I present this table to people and start talking about the importance of fantasizing in the flow-thinking paradigm, I inevitably get the question: "Isn't fantasizing bad? Shouldn't we keep our sharp business minds always rooted in reality?" In the dam-thinking world, yes, you want to stay away from fantasy because you can't move to make your dream a reality anyway. Moreover, fantasizing will just hide dangerous realities, which will create a disaster. Is dreaming a bad thing in the flow-thinking world? No; you want to spend time dreaming, because you can make your dream a reality. As a flow thinker, in order to grow, you need to dream and imagine. For example, if we fail to imagine devices such as the iPod, we get left behind. One of the reasons why Steve Jobs is a great CEO is because he imagines— he fantasizes what the world could be with a new, yet unseen product—and often Apple emerges as the only company that can deliver it. Without a dream we can't aspire to be great. Without a flow-thinking paradigm we can't realize our dream.

W. F. D. AND THE DREAM THAT CREATED GREEN GIANT

My grandfather, William F. Dietrich, started working at a small, humble company in LeSuer, Minnesota, in 1917 as a part-time bookkeeper. This company was the Minnesota Valley Canning Company, later to become the Green Giant Company. In the decades that followed, my grandfather would become president of the company and in less than ten years (back in the 1950's) lead it from a $200 million dollar company to a $2 billion dollar company. Mind you, this was done with peas and corn! Without a college education, he literally rose from poverty to affluence, from the bottom to the very top. The company started small. It grew, continued to grow, and then dominated its market. It all started with Ward Cosgrove's fantastic dream. The following is from *Memoirs of a Giant: Green Giant Company's First 75 Years, 1903 - 1978*.

> *One day in the harness shop in which the company had been started, Ward made a report to the other members of the Board. Using his Uncle Jim's safe as a podium, and with his audience seated on the piles of horse collars and blankets, he predicted that Minnesota Valley would eventually pay him $10,000 a year, have a profitable research department, breed its own seed and advertise*

as Campbell Soup did. "The meeting broke up after my report," he was to recall. "The directors wanted to get out into the fresh air, sunshine and land of realities.

I would have quiet conversations with my grandfather. He would be puffing on a cigar, sitting on a sofa or a big, comfortable leather chair. A martini glass would be close by. You never really asked my grandfather a question. You just sat there and waited, and eventually he would say something. People would often think my grandfather was snoozing, but what he was actually doing was keeping his mind in a very relaxed state—thinking. He would say something like, "Gray, you need to learn how to use the old bean," pointing to his head. Another, and a favorite, was, "business is just common sense."

My grandfather's common sense was special. For him, it was just common sense that people have to grow in order for a company to grow. So why wouldn't you encourage your people to learn and grow beyond what they could imagine? It was just common sense that a company always stayed focused on its purpose and mission. And, through that focus and delivery of your product and service, you would earn and receive a fair profit—a profit that you would invest back into your people and your company. It was just common sense if you wanted people to buy your product that you would provide the highest quality product and service possible and then stretch yourself to do better. It was just common sense that if you wanted to know what the customer thought, that you would personally go out to where the customer used the product and listen and observe. Why wouldn't you let customers tell you about the product and show you how they were using it so that you could design a better product? It was just common sense that if you wanted to have minimal operational costs, you would get everything flowing as fast as possible. Keep the flow clean. Don't let anything sit. And always invest in anything that creates higher velocity. He would say it to me like a mantra, "Gray, business is just common sense." He almost implied that anyone could run a company. He just never appreciated how special his common sense was.

My grandfather very much operated within the flow-paradigm column in the table above. He would oscillate between running his company in a very practical and realistic way, using his special brand of common sense, and then, at other times, he would spend a lot of time thinking, imagining, and dreaming. If you were a young entrepreneur, you might find a short handwritten note to meet him at a small club in town. When you met him, he might start out with, "How is business?" or, "How are the kids?" Before you knew it, you would find yourself all alone with him, in a quiet corner, or a balcony, or a small lounge. You would feel very comfortable. And then he would ask the deep question, and you wouldn't think it was deep until you began to try to answer it. He would listen, never, ever cutting you off or giving any hint of an opinion one way or the other. It wasn't uncommon to see my grandfather close his eyes as if he was sleeping while you were talking to him. If he did that you were in trouble, because what he was doing was formulating, in his almost unconscious state, the follow-up question. When you heard the follow-up question, you knew he heard absolutely every little detail you told him and understood exactly what you said. And you soon saw that the follow-up question was about a place, very far away, not based on reality, but based on imagination, a place where you would be part of a company with unlimited growth.

WHAT IS DAM THINKING?

Control. We like control. We need control. Anthropologically, it is how we overcame the uncertain nomadic life. We were once early-day *Homo sapiens* roaming around the landscape, following the great flows of the wind, sea, land, and migration. With dams we took control. Now, with the power of a dam, we become masters of the universe. With dam control, we try to stop change because we, as humans, whether we like to think this isn't so or not, hate change. For example, who is in favor of nature winning and having Venice slip into the mud and sea, forever lost? What are we doing to save it? We are creating a dam, of sorts, to control the inflows into the Venetian lagoon. We are trying to solve a problem by stopping and controlling a natural, emergent flow that is essential to the ecology of the lagoon. Said another way, in order to stop change, we are applying a complicated solution to a complex system. We do this all the time, particularly in the companies we run. Are there going to be side effects, because of our attempts to control the lagoon? You bet! The unpleasant reality is we can't stop Venice from sinking. We can't stop an earthquake, flood, volcano, or tornado. We can't stop the natural emergent flow processes that shape our world; that shape our universe. We can't even stop ourselves from change—we age. We aren't as powerful as we think! In reality, all dams are a symbol of humanity's hubris. All dams come down in time. Flow, despite what we may think, can't be stopped.

Dam thinkers like to make things big. It feeds their ego. Because of this need, dam thinkers lack any sensitivity to scale. Two common ways I see scale problems in the dam-thinking world are: one, the tragedy of the commons and two, the violation of the rule of 150. A typical example of the tragedy of the commons is where improvements to health and food are made to increase the population. The problem is that with an uncontrolled increase in the population comes a depletion of a common vital resource, such as ground water, which creates a disaster. The depletion of the common resource is why it is called the tragedy of the commons; once this *common* resource is gone, there is little or no hope of getting it back. When this happens you have a real tragedy.

In the book, *Logic of Failure,* by Dietrich Dörner, people are put in a simple simulation game. Most people going into it think they won't have a disaster. Many people, even though they know better and are well schooled in the tragedy of the commons, make decisions that create the tragedy of the commons. I cite this because people think that if they see the proof and know what to do, they will do the right thing. Guess what? They won't. They can't see the flow-thinking world when their head operates with a dam-thinking paradigm. The only way to do the right thing is to make a conscious decision to change the way they think.

You can see the tragedy of the commons dilemma in businesses. Consider a new plant manager starting out. Because he thinks he has superior powers (and this delusion feeds his ego) he starts to make decisions based on fantasy. The new manager has one laser-light thought: how can I be promoted? He decides on a number that the plant must produce and starts loading up the shop in that amount. The result is a traffic jam—a dam—created by the manager's need to feed his ego. When top management asks why the factory has such low performance and can't meet deliveries, the plant manager insists on a larger plant so that he can do the same thing and create an even bigger traffic jam at exponentially higher costs!

The manager doesn't see the problem. In fact, he sees just the opposite. Success! He is delighted with all of the work flooding the floor. The reservoir of partially completed work gives the illusion of abundant need within his plant. The resulting problems from the chaos of the traffic jam give him the feeling of abundant importance, which feeds his ego even more. He seems to think that he is the only one capable of making decisions. He is the only one capable of thinking through solutions. The ineptitude of his people feeds his sense of superior intelligence. Ironically, all the problems in the plant were created by his own dam thinking!

At some point, this plant manager exhausts the limited amount of resources of the factory plant floor, the factory workers, the factory equipment, the company's money, or all of the above! The damage is almost always completely unrecoverable; the reputation of the company is ruined. And another business and market leaves the United States and goes offshore.

Malcolm Gladwell, in *The Tipping Point,* gets at a scale problem, which dam thinkers are completely insensitive to, and that is the rule of 150. Essentially, having an employee count of greater than 150 in a business means people lose track of other people fast. Think of the dynamics and socializations of a small town of 150 versus the dynamics and socializations of a big city of four million! This breakdown destroys the "work is social" fabric of the company. At that point, the company becomes disconnected and becomes a breeding ground for dams. Gladwell comments on W. L. Gore & Associates (the makers of Gore-Tex® material and Glide® dental floss) in his book *The Tipping Point...*

Wilbert "Bill" Gore—the late founder of the company... stumbled on the principle by trial and error. "We found again and again that things get clumsy at a hundred and fifty... So 150 employees per plant became the company goal."

The simple metric Wilbert Gore devised for each division was creating a parking lot with only 150 parking places. When people started parking on the grass it was time to find another empty building, create 150 new parking spaces, and create a new business unit. If I want to know if a company has a dam-thinking culture, I simply ask how many employees they have in each of their business units. The dam most active in violation of the rule of 150 is the trust dam.

Along with the need to control and stop change as well as make things big in order to feed their ego, dam thinkers like to judge in order to feel powerful. That is why dam thinkers love the annual performance review. With it, they have the power to make everyone feel insecure and average. The annual review is done at almost every company in the United States, at great labor and management cost. The review collects a pile of information, which for the most part is useless and polluted. There is a disconnect between an actual event and how it is incorrectly remembered. Nothing screws up a feedback system, which is what a review is, more than a long wait time or lag time. The review process, by design, will create damage. For example, the manager and the employee are going to remember things differently. Because of the long lag times, the manager and employee will likely disagree, and this will start to create a trust dam.

The manifestation of dam-thinking can be felt and seen in three ways: pollution, stagnation, and pressure. If you feel the need to work more and more hours, if you feel that things aren't getting done right, if you feel stressed, then you have pressure—you are working within a dam-thinking paradigm. If you find that you need greater numbers of inspectors and quality personnel, that customers find huge variation in your workmanship, that customers are growing increasingly dissatisfied with the product you deliver, then you have pollution—you are working within a dam-thinking paradigm. If you find that things just sit—plans and product on the floor, supplies in a warehouse, etc.—and so much time has passed that you wonder whether any of it is still good, then you have stagnation—you are working within a dam-thinking paradigm.

WHAT IS FLOW THINKING?

Flow thinkers have been around for hundreds, if not thousands of years. Our founding fathers were flow thinkers. They created a highly dependent, complex, and interconnected system of government that created an economic engine that grows today without limits. Benjamin Franklin was the quintessential flow thinker. He knew about the value of organizing before Toyota— "A place for everything, everything in its place." He understood scale and the power of small things before building the Titanic or Glen Canyon Dam—"A small leak can sink a great ship." He understood dam thinking before I wrote this book: the learning dam—"Being ignorant is not so much a shame, as being unwilling to learn;" the ego dam—"He that won't be counseled can't be helped;" accountability—"He that is good for making excuses is seldom good for anything else;" and, of course, velocity—"Don't put off for tomorrow what you can do today" (stated by Thomas Jefferson, but I am sure used by Mr. Franklin as well). Nothing in this book and nothing about flow thinking is new.

Many companies are a dam mess and it doesn't take long to see it. Equipment is scattered all about without any care or forethought. Piles of product traverse the factory floor in a complex web that nobody sees or understands. Priorities shift by the hour. Engineers, operators, and workers congregate. They argue and debate endlessly. Nothing is resolved. Finger pointing is rampant. Suppliers are drawn in and blamed. Problems build. Quality drops. Stuff sits everywhere in piles. People walk back and forth, up and down, leaving and coming back, accomplishing nothing. Nobody can see the real dam problem.

When faced with this all-too-common scenario, I get people back into flow by starting with the premise that every assumption they have is false. This works because flow thinking is perpendicular to dam thinking. You think the arrangement of the equipment doesn't matter? It does matter. You think that a huge amount of material released onto the factory floor will make things go faster? It makes things go slower. You think buying more equipment and putting it on the floor will produce more product? It will produce less product. You think equipment is running at overcapacity? It is running at a fraction of its capable capacity. You think punishing employees for bad production numbers will motivate the workforce? It will not motivate the workforce. You think the workers need to work harder? They need to work less. You think people's thinking and behaviors are irrelevant to your business system? They will completely define and lead your business results. Good behavior, good results; bad behavior, bad results. You think that your people are the problem? You are the problem. You and your dam thinking.

So what is a fix? The fix I used to apply before I understood fully the real need to change people's thinking from dam to flow was to conduct a Kiazen. Kiazen comes from Toyota and their production system. In a Kiazen, a small team does many different things. They move different pieces of equipment together in something called work cells. They simplify operating procedures. Inventories are removed so that only the exact materials and tools needed are on the factory floor. The whole factory is organized so that everything is in its place. All production steps are examined: what do they do and where are they done? All non-value-added steps are removed. It isn't uncommon to take a production process of 400 steps and reduce it down to twenty steps. The result is an extremely efficient operation, but there is a problem. Improving a single operation very rarely translates into an actual, discernable business result. Also, the results are difficult to sustain because few people have converted from dam thinking to flow thinking. Because of this, I don't start with a Kiazen anymore.

Before I do a Kiazen, I bring a small team together in a very special way. By using the parallel thinking strategies of Edward Debono's Six Thinking Hats, described in Chapter 5, I get the collective team intelligence to fuse into a mastermind. What is a mastermind? We all know the saying, "two heads are better than one." The mastermind idea originates from this idea. Earl Bakken and my grandfather were lifelong masterminds. Anybody can do it, yet so few people do. Way back in 1937, at the time of the Great Depression, Napoleon Hill wrote a book called *Think and Grow Rich*. It was a compilation of ideas at that time, outlining how individuals achieved great success and wealth during their lifetimes. Andrew Carnegie recruited Hill to put this book together. Hill organized the ideas into 15 principles. The ninth principle was the Power of the Master Mind. Hill defines the mastermind simply:

Coordination of knowledge and effort, in a spirit of harmony, between two or more people, for the attainment of a definite purpose.

Hill goes on to describe Carnegie's mastermind:

Mr. Carnegie's Master Mind group consisted of a staff of approximately fifty men, with whom he surrounded himself, for the definite purpose of manufacturing and marketing steel. He attributed his entire fortune to the power he accumulated through this "Master Mind."

Carnegie was able to generate a never-ending stream of ideas, complex solutions and plans and use them to sustain growth with his mastermind.

Before the mastermind sessions, the first step is to capture the team's current thinking. A simple way to do this is to list items, such as people's behaviors, operator accountability, operator skill, preventative maintenance, quality systems, the organization of equipment, cross training, experience, etc. and have the team rank these items in order of most important to least important. Record the discussion where they explain their reasons, thereby revealing their existing paradigm. This serves as evidence for review, because people quickly forget what they used to think.

The second step is to conduct a Lean Laboratory™, which is described in Chapter 8. Record what they do in the disorganized state. Ask them for recommended improvements and record that. Then have the simulated factory reorganized into simple work cells. Film what happens and the subsequent recommended improvement discussions. Have the team again rank what they deem important.

In the next meeting, you have the team members identify the dams they experienced and how their change in thinking happened. Then you ask them to mastermind around how to conduct a Kiazen event for maximum impact. What dams need to be tackled first? What complex solutions would be most appropriate? Essentially, the Kiazen itself becomes a complex plan derived from the parallel thinking of the mastermind. Complex planning is discussed in Chapter 10.

What do you do if you find some people who won't give up their dam-thinking? If you want a flow-thinking culture you cannot tolerate pollution and dam-thinking is pollution. If workers decide not to change their thinking after seeing all of the evidence and experiencing the positive benefits of flow, you will have to fire them.

Flow is about velocity, quality, and emergence. Flow thinking and dam-thinking are mutually exclusive—they are perpendicular to each other. They can't exist together in equilibrium. Despite what some think, you can't try out flow-thinking and keep dam-thinking. If you establish a flow improvement in your company, such as a quality-improvement event, or what typically is known as a Kiazen event, and you wonder why the initial outstanding improvements didn't last, it is because the dam-thinking of the company culture washed out the localized flow improvement.

The manifestation of flow-thinking can be felt and seen in three ways: velocity, quality, and emergence. If you observe that everything is getting done fast with little effort, if you observe your people constantly improvising around roadblocks, if you observe people are operating with a very low level of stress, then you have velocity—you are working within a flow-thinking paradigm. If you observe workers setting high standards, if you observe everyone is constantly communicating about everything happening around them in efforts to not make mistakes, and customers are very satisfied with the product and service they receive, then you have quality—you are working within a flow-thinking paradigm. If you observe your people coming up almost spontaneously with new ways to design and manufacture products, you observe your people coming up with totally unexpected, but very good, new ways to conduct your business that dramatically reduces costs, and you observe your people discovering new untapped markets that could be made available through some creative engineering, then you have emergence— you are working within a flow-thinking paradigm.

W. F. D. AND FLOW THINKING

In order to understand what flow feels and looks like, consider the real-time cost accounting system my grandfather (known as W. F. D. in his day) designed and implemented back in the 1950's at Green Giant. He noticed that every summer when Green Giant launched into full production mode, there were many out-of-work schoolteachers. Teachers were smart, observant, capable of adding numbers, and willing to work for little pay, so he hired a whole bunch of them. He put several in strategic locations throughout each factory. They were to note, for example, the amount of cans used, the amount of work time spent on a machine, how much product was scrapped, how much maintenance work was done on a machine—all of it by shift. He would have special sheets prepared for them so that the information could be carefully filled out and tabulated.

Workers weren't interrupted; they kept working and focused on their job. But before too long, they all started talking to each other—the workers and the teachers. The workers canned the vegetables, and the schoolteachers stood over their shoulders, watched, counted, and tabulated in real time! Their results for the operation were summarized. These were sent on to corporate where they would be tabulated for each product, each operation, each plant, and each shift. In the morning, my grandfather would have a single sheet of paper lying on his desk that would tell him if he made money the previous day. But he would also see something else.

By doing this simple thing with the schoolteachers, he had a whole bunch of smart brains observing everything that was going on! He knew about the pollution that was being fed to his production stream and stopped it. He knew what was breaking down and interrupting the flow, and stopped it. He knew what product was being scrapped and why, and stopped it. With all of the observations being made, everything was allowed to flow. And he wouldn't stay put in his office. He would take the summary pages and his own simple tabulation sheet and visit all of the plants every weekend and see for himself. Because of this, he could always see very deeply into the numbers. Because of this, Green Giant ran much more efficiently than any of its competitors. As a result, they grew fast and made a lot of money.

STORY POINT 3:
Fix the Traffic Jam with a No Rework Policy

Many plants suffer from traffic jams generated by a plant manager who has an ego dam. He or she will not ask for help to improve operational efficiencies, and that is a very bad sign. So much so, that I have often found a proud manager sitting in front of the dam constipated mess as proof of their need to expand and get big. If you buy into their story and let them have more equipment, more employees, and a bigger plant, then you will have a bigger traffic jam. Did making a freeway wider really solve a rush hour problem in any city?

Rework consumes capacity. Think of a freeway: as you add more cars, the lanes start to get more crowded. As the crowding continues, traffic begins to slow. And as more cars enter, the traffic eventually stops. The same thing happens in a plant. Rework kills capacity because it shrinks the number of traffic lanes available as work returns back into the factory.

For a client who had a manager who was proud of his constipated mess, we instituted a policy of no rework. This put enormous pressure on the manager. Rework parts were obvious, so there was no way to cheat. As the rate of scrap started to rise rapidly, the manager was forced to start asking for help. He didn't care where it came from—whether it was a supplier, an operator, an engineer, or a peer. He was in trouble and he knew it. And he knew he had to motivate people to help him, because if they didn't help him, he was done for. He was made completely dependent on others and needed to learn fast how to get people to work with him. Of course, his first tactic was to appeal to anyone who would listen to stop the no rework policy. Nobody caved into the feelings dam, fortunately.

I show on the spider diagram below that the first dam that fell with the no rework policy was the ego dam. The no rework policy forced the manager to admit that there were problems that he needed immediate help with.

Figure 4: "No Rework" Spider Diagram

The spider diagram above shows how a policy of no rework breaks the ego dam. The no rework policy, makes every mistake visible. People will have to perform at a high level. There will be no hiding places. This will expose all the weaknesses. If a manager is smart, he or she will ask for help. If managers don't ask for help, and should, then their evaluation (Story Point 2) will show an active ego dam that will need to be addressed immediately.

CHAPTER 3

A Real Dam Problem

If you can find something that everyone agrees on, it's wrong.

—Mo Udall

As I stood outside of Beehive Circuits and looked up at the thickly snow-coated Wasatch Mountains with my pipette in one hand and beaker in the other, I had no idea I was looking at what would become one of the greatest natural disasters of recent decades. It would also offer a striking analogy for the problems that existed within Beehive and many other companies entangled in dam-thinking. The way the dam nearly failed shows us the raw power of flow—a power we can choose to use if we give up dam-thinking. With the 1983 snow melt, the designers, engineers, and operators of the Glen Canyon dam found that they were faced with a real dam problem. Either the flow was going to rip down the dam or the dam designers were going to figure out how to divert and weaken the flow. A large dam and a strong flow cannot coexist at the same place at the same time without creating damage.

About half of all the water that comes off of the Rocky Mountains flows to and through the mighty Colorado River. When the snow started to melt that spring, the water flowed down into Bountiful, through North Salt Lake, into Salt Lake City, then into Sandy as streets flooded. I remember Bill Rowsell looking me in the eyes and saying, "Lake Bonneville is returning!"—and he meant it. Lake Bonneville was an ancient lake of mostly fresh water that was about 325 miles long, 135 miles wide, and over 1,000 feet deep. Roughly the size of Lake Superior, it was created by the melting of glaciers and snow from the last ice age.

In 1963, the Glen Canyon Dam was completed and water began filling into what is now Lake Powell. This lake reached the *full pool* stage in 1980, creating a vast reservoir that is the second largest in the United States. In 1983, deep winter snows resulted in spring runoff from the mountains into Lake Powell at about 110,000 cubic feet per second. To get an idea of the scale of this water flow, the Metrodome in Minneapolis contains 60 million cubic feet of air, which is the same volume as approximately 3,300 average size homes. This inflow into Lake Powell would have filled the Metrodome in about nine minutes!

The Glen Canyon Dam is a massive structure: 1,560 feet long, 710 feet high, with a base 310 feet wide at the bottom. The dam required over 132 million cubic feet of concrete to complete. To help you visualize the dam scale, this would be over two Metrodomes completely filled to the top with concrete. When you build big, people anticipate a great benefit. In reality—and what you will see in Chapter 6—when we build big, the great disaster is only a razor's edge away. Disaster may come from a single scrape against an iceberg, which is what sunk the Titanic. It may come from a single, very large order that didn't materialize, which is what happened with Beehive. It may come from a larger than expected snow melt coming off the Rocky Mountains.

DAM WASTE

Anytime you stop the flow of a stream of water, or information, or cars on a freeway, or material moving on a factory floor, you will have stagnation, pollution, and pressure. One of the consequences of creating Lake Powell is that it loses much more water through evaporation than the flowing river ever did. It is estimated that the yearly water loss over what would naturally occur without the lake is equivalent to the amount used by 900,000 people per year. Often, this water loss is reported as a very small annual percent, such as a 1 percent loss above what would be expected from the flowing river. The fact, though, is that the small percentage of evaporative water loss out of Lake Powell is equivalent to the annual drinking demands of 900,000 people. No matter how you might spin it, that is a lot of water! That is why scale is so important. If the dam was upstream, creating a reservoir one quarter as big, the evaporative water loss would be much less. Scale and location matter!

But that isn't all of the loss of water from Lake Powell. Dam experts seemed to ignore the significance that the rock walls in Glen Canyon are thirsty—the rock is very porous. Porous rock has many small voids where water can be easily absorbed into the rock. The amount of water lost into the porous sandstone and limestone walls of Lake Powell represents enough water for 2,500,000 people per year! In total, the amount of water lost, just from the water sitting still and being stagnant, represents enough drinking water for 3.1 million people per year! The irony of these facts is that the dam isn't conserving water; it is losing it! Dam thinking often produces results opposite of what was intended.

Let's look at yet another dam issue. The Glen Canyon dam not only dams up water, but all of the sediment that comes down off the mountain. The natural flow of the Colorado is warm, muddy, and still as it enters Lake Powell. The current flow below the dam is cold and clear. The dam has changed the ecosystem of the river and the canyon. It is predicted that in 300–500 years, Lake Powell will be so full of sediment that the reservoir will be unusable.

THEORY FAILS TO ANTICIPATE
THE REAL DAM PROBLEM

Two of the pioneers of chemical reactor engineering are Neal R. Amundson and Rutherford Aris, and in many ways they were single-handedly responsible for making chemical engineering such a mathematically rigorous field. Moreover, the models that they created, which are used to design highly efficient flow based reactors, are the principle reason why all chemical engineers have a bias for flow processes. During my chemical engineering training at the University of Minnesota at Amundson Hall, I would marvel at the way Mr. Aris could so easily explain the rudimentary application of the Laplace Transform. Mr. Aris made everything so obvious and simple that you thought you were having a casual conversation with someone at Starbucks. Whereas Mr. Aris gave me a feeling of hope, Matthew Tirrell gave me feelings of utter despair.

Matthew Tirrell, a gifted, young engineering professor, was my fluid dynamics professor back in 1982. Today he is the dean of chemical engineering at the University of California–Santa Barbara. Mr. Tirrell looked somewhat like a rock star, big hair and an attitude, but sporting a tie and modern sport jacket. This strange juxtaposition would catch all of our eyes as he walked swiftly into the large lecture hall and started rattling off concepts, formulas, derivations, and examples, while everyone was furiously taking notes. About halfway through, almost to the minute of each lecture, he would realize that what he had done was wrong! There would be a long pause. A chilled silence filled the hall. Pencils frozen. Eyes were glued. And minds were filled with, "Oh no, not again." Matt would say, "No, that isn't right," and chalk dust would fly as he started to erase whole sections of the board. We would all look at each other. Frustrated and scared, "If he can't get it, how could we?"

What we were trying to learn in his class was how to apply the famous Navier-Stokes equations. This set of equations explains the fluid flow for any given situation. The problem is that they are so difficult to solve that you have to make all sorts of assumptions and cross out all sorts of terms. For example, you assume that something really large doesn't change much and that something really small is totally insignificant. When you keep making those sorts of assumptions you end up with something you can solve: the perfect analytical solution (*analytic* means perfectly solvable with no noise and completely predictable). Perfection is a beautiful thing in mathematics, but mathematics is abstract, not real. Much of our education in many fields focuses on the perfect solution, which is, by the way, fantasy. It is necessary to understand the perfect solution, but it is also necessary to understand that the real world isn't nice, clean, and perfect.

We treasure analytical solutions so much that when data contradicts the model, we love to ignore it and focus on the fantasy that the equation is still perfect. This is a bad behavior, yet it is taught in many of the best schools. As chemical engineers, we saw this in our unit operations laboratory. Part of the laboratory was to derive the theoretical result. The other part was to test the theory against the real result by operating a real machine, such as an evaporator or a distillation tower. Almost always there were significant differences between the theoretical result and the real world result, and this should have revealed something very important to me and my classmates. Instead of trying to rationalize the errors and twist reality into a well-composed answer, which you might read in a text book, we should have been focusing on what we didn't know and learn how to discover new and interesting things. If we had done that, we would have gained valuable insights about the real world and the nature of complex problems.

This brings us back to the dam and the problem with the rising water level of Lake Powell in the spring of 1983. The spillways were designed using the equations I learned in 1982— the Navier-Stokes equations. The engineers and designers never had the spillways tested at theoretical maximum capacity. They should have, because, when they were first operated at full capacity, they quickly failed. How could such smart people make such a bad decision? The usual rationalization goes something like this: "My time is so valuable, and the likelihood that full capacity would ever be required so rare, that to do the test would be so meaningless and prove to be such a tremendous waste of my time that I don't see why I needed to bother with it. I will just skip it."

Consider the Chernobyl disaster on April 26, 1986. At Chernobyl, the engineers thought they could run the reactor well outside of the design limits in order to shorten the time for experiments designed to check systems, ironically, for safer reactor operation. They didn't know that they were in serious trouble until a few minutes before they blew themselves up, destroyed the building, contaminated the town, and sent a huge radiation cloud all over central Europe that affected the lives of millions of people.

Disasters such as this always have an ego dam lurking in the background. The ego dam creates an attitude that the rules don't apply. We are special. You see this with CEOs, professional athletes, and politicians. Who could forget Richard Nixon saying in the David Frost interview, "When the President does it, that means that it's not illegal." Ego dams are destructive. Our behaviors are governed by our thinking. Behaviors lead results.

And it was way too late for the Glen Canyon Dam! With 110,000 cubic feet per second of water coming into the lake, the spillways had to run at maximum capacity. If not, the water in Lake Powell would overtake the dam. After a few days, the dam began to vibrate horribly. Down in its belly, people thought they were in a war zone. Rebar, concrete, and great slabs of rock were shooting out of the spillways. When the water in the left spillway was shut down and examined, it was found that the three-foot-thick wall of steel-reinforced concrete had been eroded all the way through and continued into the rock! When flow was resumed, it was estimated that rock was being eroded away at 1,000 tons per second! At one point, it was feared that so much rock would be eroded away that the plug at the bottom of the spillway, which prevents Lake Powell from draining, would fail. That would cause a catastrophic drain of Lake Powell. Glen Canyon Dam was squarely centered in the disaster quadrant. When the flow into the lake slowed and the spillways could be shut down, inspection of the left spillway revealed a gigantic crater-sized hole some 80-feet wide and over 30-feet deep!

THE VERY SMALL CAN DESTROY
THE VERY LARGE

What was causing the Glen Canyon Dam to fail? Near the end of the fluid dynamics course that I took in Amundson Hall was a short, messy section describing cavitation. Cavitation is a chaotic phenomenon that requires all sorts of empirical approaches (*empirical* can sometimes mean guessing and then watching what happens). If you were to run a spoon through a pot full of caramel quickly, you would notice the spoon pulling apart the caramel and creating a cavity behind it. This isn't cavitation, but the analogy is a simple illustration of its effects. When you run a surface—such as a propeller surface—through water really fast, or run water over a surface in a flow very fast, the water can separate itself from the surface it is flowing over. What causes the separation is often nothing more than a little surface roughness or inconsistency. The small amount of separation from the surface creates small, vacuum-like water vapor bubbles. As these move to higher pressure areas away from the surface, they compress. At this point, the temperature in the bubble can reach over 1,000 degrees Fahrenheit! As the bubbles compress, they start to descend toward the surface of the concrete. As the energy of the bubble and the weight of the bubble increase and get closer to the concrete surface (in the case of a spillway) they implode, creating a very powerful shock wave. This small shock wave removes just a small amount of concrete. This, in turn, produces more cavitation, and creates more holes in the concrete, until powerful water jets start blasting away and cutting through the concrete and steel. Eventually, normal erosion processes take over and create the large craters and damage that ultimately render the spillways useless.

What was the solution to the cavitation problem? The bubbles were not allowed to self-organize and explode near the surface concrete. A ramp was built about half way down the spillway. This ramp launched the water up, causing air to mix with the water (aeration, in engineering terms) so that the few cavitation bubbles that remained could explode harmlessly, well away from the surface concrete.

In companies embarking on flow-thinking ideas, I like to think of their small, high-performance teams as cavitation bubbles. They are small, but powerful. They make real discoveries and implement change quickly. As a result, the company starts to change around them. If you have dam-thinking managers, these teams will be stopped because they are a threat and the team is easy to stop. That is why, if you really want a flow-thinking culture, you have to hold your managers to high standards of behavior and evaluate their performance against those behaviors, not against their claimed results that might not be real. The need for evaluations is stressed in Chapter 4.

YOU CAN'T SEE FLOW-THINKING WITH A DAM-THINKING MIND

So often, companies operating with a dam-thinking paradigm want me to prove to them with numbers and statistics that flow thinking works. There is nothing I can show them to get them to believe. For example, I may show them huge productivity improvements that took place, but they still reject the notion that work is social. Their dam-thinking paradigm rejects the notion that something so significant could come from getting people to work better together. Data and experiments and half efforts won't get you to see flow-thinking. You have to get there by challenging your existing thought processes. In order to make the big leap into flow-thinking, you will need to make a leap of faith—you will need to believe that a flow has to be better than a dam.

In Barry Oshry's book, *Seeing Systems: Unlocking the Mysteries of Organizational Life,* we see examples of flow-thinking colliding with dam-thinking. Oshry gets different people from different companies, from the mail room all the way to the executive level, to participate in his event at his retreat. Upon getting off the bus, you are assigned a bottom, middle, or top position. Before too long, you have a fictional company that is borderline between dysfunctional and disaster. The resulting behavior is all too real. In one event, a customer wanted to select her own people from within the company and form her own team where she, as the customer, would be a member! The company resisted strongly, from middle management to the top. They saw her as an interference and a pushy person. But she persisted. "She insists on being right in there with the workers" (93). The other customers didn't get the product they wanted on time or on budget. They felt righteously screwed. She, on the other hand, changed the ground rules. She took responsibility for the production and delivery of her product. And she got a high-quality product on time and on budget. She was very satisfied. How was she perceived by the company?

> *Through one set of lenses, we see a pattern of personal behavior: pushiness, over control, lack of trust, and so forth. Through another set of lenses, we see a person transforming the predictable Provider/Customer dance. (94)*

What she was to the supplier company was a threat—a cavitation bubble that threatened the foundation of the dam upon which the people at the company had grown dependent. What she was doing was not going to be repeated. It would be an aberration that could be ignored. Yet, what she did was about ten years ahead of what later became known as a SCRUM team (see the next section and Story Point 8 on page 133 for a good description of SCRUM). SCRUM is a proven, highly powerful way to manage projects using flow-thinking. The challenge with SCRUM is that it starts to destroy a company's dam-thinking culture. The result is a war that, left unchecked, can destroy a company that fails to make the decision to stop flow and go back to dam-thinking, or tear down dam-thinking and move toward flow-thinking. You can't have flow-thinking and dam-thinking going on at the same time for very long without some serious damage taking place.

SCRUM: PROJECT MANAGEMENT THAT RIPS DOWN DAM-THINKING

A very inefficient project management system was used to design the Glen Canyon Dam. The designers didn't have a choice. The scale of the dam was just too big. You couldn't build part of a full-scale dam, see something you don't like, change it, and build another version of the dam at full scale! A big dam, like all big things, is an all-or-nothing affair. Was Howard Hughes certain his Spruce Goose would fly? You have to know everything about a gigantic dam—or, for that matter, a gigantic anything—before you design and build it. If you miss something, well, too bad.

The project management system used for the Glen Canyon Dam is called *waterfall*. Think of a bunch of dams with a small amount of water dribbling over the top with a barely discernable flow rate. The reservoir for the first dam in waterfall is all of the specifications and requirements that the customer wants. And it has to be everything, because once you start the design step, you can't go back and add any new features! The amount of time you have to wait to complete each step of the waterfall, the huge, complicated pile of detail and information, and the inability to loop back and make corrections to a previous step makes this project management strategy a dam nightmare—a system that often produces disasters because it is entirely based on dam-thinking. It is a system that requires perfect knowledge, with no room to learn anything new. And yet, it is the project management system of choice by many companies across many industries today. Even companies that know and have used SCRUM with success!

For projects of a more reasonable scale, think of SCRUM like a water jet shooting out at high speed, instead of a huge, overflowing reservoir slowly dribbling over a dam. SCRUM is all about flow. Almost all software companies used to develop buggy software that was expensive, late, and didn't have the functionality customers really wanted. SCRUM fixed that. SCRUM was formulated by Ken Schwaber and Jeff Sutherland to help software companies develop new products with a predictable schedule, budget, and performance. A SCRUM operates with a small cross functional team that has to deliver product within a tight time box called a *sprint*. The product delivered has very specific, but limited functionality. Functionality is added with each successive sprint until the customer is satisfied. I rarely have had to go much past four sprints in manufacturing design and development projects before a customer is satisfied. A project managed using SCRUM may take two to four months, instead of one to two years using waterfall.

The SCRUM process minimizes planning, maximizes action, maximizes learning, and demands iteration and improvisation. SCRUM will force you to deal with immediate reality, because there just isn't any tolerance for waiting in SCRUM. The best SCRUMs happen when you have highly skilled, motivated people. SCRUMs perform miserably if you have people with poor skill sets and bad behaviors. This is because SCRUM is a flow process. Flows have little tolerance for pollution of any kind, be it people, materials, tools, goals, communication, or behaviors. Because SCRUM is a flow process, you will see the pollution immediately, and you will have to fix it fast or simply go back to the waterfall paradigm knowing that you and your company are doomed. For this reason, even though SCRUM is highly effective, it isn't necessarily popular—and you can easily find people who will talk very badly about SCRUM. If they do, you know right away that they are dam-thinkers.

Daily meetings make SCRUM work. They drive things forward, almost as if each day were a crisis. The leader of the SCRUM, the SCRUM master, updates something called the burn down chart. It shows the units of work remaining daily. The burn down chart makes the velocity of the team transparent. Within only a few days, the team members, as well as management, know whether things are on time and on budget. And because the customer is also on the team, the customer knows too! Waterfall encourages excuses, lack of accountability, lack of commitment, and procrastination. This is all eliminated with SCRUM. SCRUM absolutely demands quality and drives projects to completion fast.

STORY POINT 4:
The Power of Designed Experiments over Perfect Analytical Models

There are very successful companies that spend a lot of money working with very smart people, with very sophisticated models, and with very large and powerful computer systems. I attended a talk at the JMP Users Conference at SAS Institute headquarters in Cary, North Carolina, some years ago (JMP is a powerful flow-thinking product, it is also a visual centric data analysis package). An engineering director at Procter & Gamble explained how they worked with the scientists at Los Alamos National Laboratories to help them with the design of their shampoo bottles and potato chips (Pringles). The equations used to design a bottle that doesn't break when dropped from great heights, or to design a potato chip so that it is aerodynamic as it is shot into the can at almost supersonic speeds and stacks perfectly without breaking, are not simple; the equations are messy. The models involve hundreds of equations with thousands of inputs all feeding off of each other iteratively in a technique known as *finite element analysis*. They are messy because the real world is messy. You can't discount the effect of the very large. You can't discount the effect of the very small. You can't discount the effect of anything in between! This means that your power to predict, using analytical-based equations, is much more limited and a lot more expensive than you ever imagined. All of this gets exponentially worse as things get big! When you build an analytical model from scratch, it assumes you completely understand the system. Operating with only current knowledge isn't always good or efficient.

Throughout my career, I became adept at solving problems in which I had very little experience and knowledge; in fact, sometimes I knew nothing. Some of my PhD colleagues who saw my approach and the way I discovered new things thought I was *cheating* because I didn't understand the system I was studying!

Some really smart people look at problem solving as a highly cerebral, singular, introverted activity. That is why so many companies really wonder about the value of highly educated PhDs in the real world of new products and new process development. Work is social. A mastermind of young, smart kids fresh out of school with undergraduate degrees will likely outperform the lone PhD that lives in a tight silo.

A designed experiment (DOE and stated as the letters D, O, E and not the word DOE) is one of those tools that allows someone with very little experience and knowledge to learn about a system's behaviors at warp speed. A DOE consists of runs. For each run, you change a number of things in order to create a result. The things you change are called variables, such as concentrations, rate settings, temperatures, pressures, etc. The results you measure, called responses, include yield, cost, quality, production speed, thicknesses, variations, etc. The mathematical machinery used for designed experiments generates a model based purely on the data, and it has nothing to do with physics or science or anything else. The key is keeping the DOEs small and focused so that they can be done quickly, which will accelerate learning. If you have a substantial problem, you should create a flow of DOEs of some three to four in succession. I have never had to perform more than four full-blown DOEs to solve any problem I have encountered in industry. The power of DOEs is in uncovering how the different variables affect or depend on each other: the dependencies or interactions. DOEs uncover dependencies very efficiently. DOEs, if done right, are extremely powerful and efficient.

What I show in the spider diagram that follows is that the learning dam falls first when you implement a designed experiment. If you do it right, discoveries are almost immediate. It is important to document everything you observe while performing a DOE, as you will see when I discuss the October Surprise described in Chapter 5.

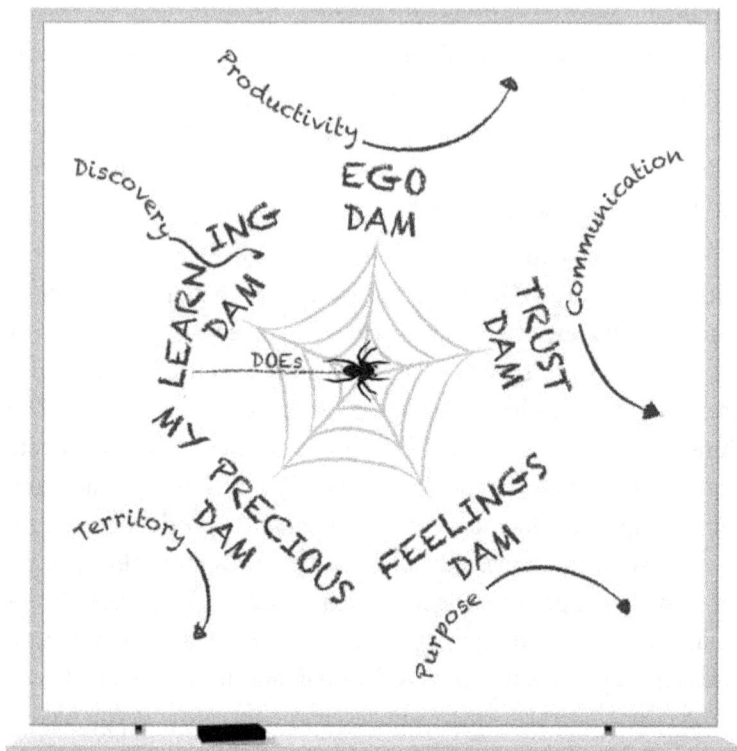

Figure 5: "Design of Experiments (DOEs)" Spider Diagram

DOEs force people to look at the real world. Because, almost always, well-planned and well-scaled DOEs produce unanticipated results, new discoveries are generated. These surprises lead to more study, research, and experiments. DOEs are a great foundation for any company that wants to be a learning organization.

CHAPTER 4

What Causes People to Hate Their Job?

Letting your customers set your standards is a dangerous game, because the race to the bottom is pretty easy to win. Setting your own standards—and living up to them—is a better way to profit.

—Seth Godin

I remember a number of times riding with my dad in the car and hearing him say, "Son, I don't know why people get unhappy working in a company." Are the people in your company unhappy? Do they hate their job? Should you care? When I moved from Beehive Circuits in Salt Lake City, Utah, to Photocircuits in Glen Cove, Long Island, New York, I really didn't know what I was doing. Fortunately, I was 24. It was a great time in my life to take a risk and do something way over my head. I had good times there, but within a short period of time I became overwhelmed and increasingly discouraged. The experience taught me a few very valuable lessons, as you will see in this chapter. Though I am very grateful for the experience, and grateful how Photocircuits propelled my career forward like a rocket, it is an experience I never want to repeat—one of those *learning* opportunities we all seem to have at least once in our lives.

I remember loading up my truck with my few belongings and starting the long drive to New York. I drove to the city on a Sunday. As I passed Paramus, New Jersey, I noticed the homes looked different, the freeways started to open up into more lanes, and I began to think the stories about New York were an exaggeration, because I was within 50 miles of the city and couldn't see it yet. In the Midwest where I grew up, you could see a city from a very long way away. The drive had been very quiet with few cars, and I thought the worries from my parents about whether I should be doing this at all were all unfounded. Suddenly, there was traffic all over the place and a huge traffic jam in front of the George Washington Bridge. To give you an idea of how naive I was, I thought there was only one bridge in New York City, the Brooklyn Bridge!

My dad used to tell people, as a joke, "I am just a simple country boy trying to make good in the big city " and the big city he was talking about was Minneapolis or what some call the Minne-Apple. I was in the Big Apple! At that moment, I felt like a poor country boy just trying to survive the day! After I paid the toll, a process new to me, I entered the bridge, which was a labyrinth of cones, dust, workers, equipment, and holes where I could see all the way down to the Hudson River below. The bridge was under massive construction, which in New York City included work on Sundays. And even with massive reconstruction, you just couldn't completely shut down such a vital bridge.

After I emerged from the dust and debris of the bridge a sign read, "Welcome to the Bronx." I had watched movies such as *Fort Apache, The Bronx,* and I never visualized myself in this place. I was on the Cross-Bronx expressway and terrified out of my mind. I looked high above, from the canyon of the expressway, to see a rail car pass above me covered in graffiti and I thought, "This is just like the movies." I passed a few burned shells of cars and wondered why nobody had removed them. I didn't know that if you got a flat on the Cross-Bronx and walked away to call somebody to help, you would have your car stripped and burned in just a few minutes.

I didn't appreciate it at the time, but I was learning a very important life lesson that would later prove to be a big part of the answer to the question, "How do you make a company great?" That life lesson was the profound effect of environment and context on my behavior. In *The Tipping Point,* Gladwell speaks to this:

> *When it comes to interpreting other people's behavior, human beings invariably make the mistake of overestimating the importance of fundamental character traits and underestimating the importance of the situation and context (160).*

My whole being was literally being changed by the very scary environment of the Bronx. I felt like I needed a gun, lots of guns. If someone were to be hurt on the road, I likely wouldn't stop, I would move on. If some people tried to stop my car, I would likely run them over. I felt threatened. I felt like an animal. People react strongly to their environment, the rules of the road, and what other people around them are doing. That is why peer pressure always outweighs parental pressure. If you encourage your kids to be involved with positive activities with positive people in positive environments with lots of support, then you have a really good chance of having really good kids. Bad parents are simply those that don't care about the who, what, where, or when of their kids, especially during the critical time when they are teenagers.

The problem with the Bronx was that nobody cared. The standards of what were acceptable were set incredibly low. I saw piles of rubble, tattered buildings, and broken windows. In his book, *The Tipping Point*, Gladwell talks about how the application of the theory of broken windows caused New York City to go from one of the most dangerous places to live to one of the safest places to live. The theory goes something like this: if you are in a city and you come across a broken window, you wonder why someone didn't have it replaced. Then you think it is because nobody cares. This means that if you wanted, you could break a window too. And if you broke a window and went inside and took something, would anyone care? And so it goes with ever-escalating crime. What this theory means is that if you crack down on one simple thing, such as broken windows, and set a standard, such as "no broken windows allowed," this will change the behavior of the population.

Did this really work? Yes it did. First, no subway cars were allowed to have graffiti. If a subway car had graffiti, then it was cleaned—practically on the spot—or taken off the system. Second, if you jumped the turnstiles in order to board a subway without paying you were arrested on the spot, lined up in chains, and processed through a mobile police station. Third, no forced window washing was allowed on the streets. When I lived in New York and drove into the city and stopped at a light, somebody would come up to my car, wash my windows, and then demand payment. All of these people were arrested. These seemingly insignificant and simple things proved to be the powerful force that drove the crime rate down very rapidly. If you think about this with an open mind, you will see this is just common sense. Criminals don't like getting arrested for doing really minor things.

They either have to stop a life of crime or go somewhere else. Like my grandfather said, "Business is just using common sense!" You need to keep your business and your factories clean. You need to hold your people to a high standard. You must not accept broken windows.

Watch the movie *Patton*. He understood the importance of holding everyone accountable for the little things that define the standard of a good soldier. Patton knew which battles were important and could not be lost. He would not lose the battle of a good looking, clean soldier with all of his gear ship-shape— period! No compromise, no excuses allowed. You must not lose the battle of broken windows with your kids. You must not lose the battle of broken windows with your company.

THE ABSOLUTE, ESSENTIAL NEED FOR ACCOUNTABILITY

What does this have to do with happy employees? Everything. People get anxious when they don't understand the standards of a company—standards of how everything in your company is organized, how everything is to be kept clean, how meetings should be conducted, and how your teams are expected to perform. When managers try to manage people by relating to their employees on psychological terms (which results in negative feelings) they will fail miserably. They make employees feel even worse. Yet many managers get mixed up in lengthy therapy sessions they are unqualified to conduct. They get completely entangled in the feelings dam and the whole purpose of their job, their department, and their company. If you insist on keeping managers around who are enmeshed with the feelings dam, the business purpose of your company will become lost forever. The way to make employees happy is to set standards and make people accountable to those standards.

What is quality? Do you remember the question for which nobody had the right answer at Beehive in Chapter 1? Quality is so important. Without quality you have nothing. Quality is holding yourself, your team, your customer, and your company to a high standard in which everyone is accountable for achieving that standard. If you want to increase the quality, raise the standards in your company. If you want your kids to be better, raise the standard and make your kids accountable to that standard. If you just put them to the test, you will be amazed at how happy that makes them and amazed at what they can accomplish. Yes, there will be complaining. Yes, there will be periods of stress and pain. Yes, you may wonder if you should cave into their feelings and start to let things slip. In the end, though, your people will see the Promised Land, and they will become tremendously loyal to your company.

PSYCHO—CIRCUS!

As I drove along the Cross-Bronx Expressway, I eventually came to the Throgs Neck Bridge on my way to Long Island. At the top of the bridge, I could see a long length of the island of Manhattan, with buildings upon buildings, cars surrounding me, and people everywhere. I wondered, "What have I done?" I wasn't in Kansas anymore, that was for sure.

When I arrived at my new job, I was told how things work. I was responsible for all imaging operations related to screen printing. This was the first time, but not the last time, that I was assigned a job I knew absolutely nothing about and had no idea where to begin. Moreover, I don't think I wanted to know about screen printing. It sounded like something I would have done if I hadn't gone to college. I was beginning to think that maybe that beaker and pipette with the mountain view back in Salt Lake City wasn't such a bad place.

The president of the company at the time—and, later, the owner of Photocircuits—was John Endee. New Yorkers love to talk. They love to talk about their city, and, in John's case, he loved to talk about himself. The bravado of such talk energizes New Yorkers, but it went against the modesty I had been taught in my Midwest upbringing. I absolutely didn't understand John, and it was clear from my first meeting to my last meeting with him that nothing went well. We were too different.

Every morning I would wake up and X off a day on my calendar. I really hated going to work. It was cramped, dirty, noisy, and crazy. I sometimes called the place the *psycho-circus*. When I arrived at work, I would hear my name being paged, just as I was getting out of my car, on the massive intercom system that was loud and blaring. "Gray McQuarrie, 2345, Gray McQuarrie 2345." Yes, there was a large megaphone speaker perched on top of the building! I sometimes wondered what those rich Wall Street people thought of my name at the Glen Cove Country Club right next door! The barrage was constant and 70 percent of the time it was for the engineers. I would walk into the processing area and be bombarded with problems that needed immediate attention. I was like a chicken running around with its head cut off each and every day and, at the same time, I was expected to get projects done that would improve the process. If I focused on the floor, my boss would be extremely unhappy because I wasn't getting project work done. If I focused on the projects then my boss would be unhappy because I wasn't helping the people on the floor. If I multitasked, I wasn't focused enough. If I focused, then I needed to learn to multitask. It was a living, breathing nightmare. I had no idea what was expected of me or the standards to which I was held. But if someone was unhappy with me, I was in trouble—be it a product manager, a supervisor on the floor, an operator, my boss, or John Endee. Managing just how one person felt was hard enough, but a whole plant! It is a wonder I didn't crack up!

My performance level and what was expected on any given day was ambiguous at best. Chronic ambiguity in any company is a bad thing. Ambiguity can stop companies from growing! Back in May 2004, I interviewed for the director of global business process improvement (DGBPI) at Dell's corporate headquarters. As impressive as that sounds, a director-level position really doesn't mean much at Dell. There were something like seven levels of vice presidents, and there were a lot of them at the time of my interview. Beehive could have been a Dell, but they lacked the vision and commitment Michael Dell had. Dell grew fast, but was what they were doing sustainable?

Dell corporate headquarters is located in low, large, concrete warehouse structures in Round Rock, Texas, just outside of Austin. It looks like a bunch of Walmarts all pushed together. The interview process I had there was strange. Everyone told me about the desire to make Dell one of the biggest companies in the world. The big goal, as you will see in Chapter 6: Scale-Up Insanity, isn't a very good goal. Today, Dell has $52.9 billion in revenue with an EBITDA of $3.62 billion. Compare that to Medtronic's $15 billion in revenue with an EBITDA of over $5 billion. Dell's low earnings suggest dams, and with dams comes dam-thinking. And that is what I saw in my interview.

There were two things said to me over and over again during the interview. One was that they were going to compete with Hewlett Packard on price, especially on printers, which had me completely baffled. Printers? Make the biggest commodity item more of a commodity! The second thing went something like this, "Kevin (Rollins) and Michael (Dell) say we have to learn how to deal with ambiguity." Nothing is worse than having ambiguity in a large company. Ambiguity is the breeding ground for all dam-thinking. You will have people behaving very badly, fighting against each other, being extremely political, and not doing any meaningful work in a culture that values ambiguity!

I didn't impress Dell; I wasn't what they were looking for and I didn't like anything I heard or saw in them. I wanted to go with a company that was growing in value. Since 2004, Dell went from about a 50 dollar per share stock price to a 13 dollar per share price today. Dell is not a flow company, they are a dam company. In my opinion, they are a mess. Behaviors and thinking lead results. For a long time now, Dell's results have failed to impress Wall Street.

Returning back to Photocircuits and their culture of ambiguity. What I was living in was a massive reservoir created by the dam mindset that wanted product slammed onto the floor in every nook, cranny, and space that could be found. Photocircuits was a massive traffic jam. Armies of expeditors would devise ways to move the product. As I quickly found out, engineers, like me, were hired to improve the quality without touching the dam system that John Endee and his dam management team had devised. The engineers were under constant pressure. Pollution, which was blamed on the engineers and not the system, was everywhere. Nothing was moving and everything was stagnant. I was, needless to say, very unhappy with my life!

THROWING AWAY THE FEELINGS DAM!

One morning I looked at myself in the mirror and said, "That's it, I am going to do something completely different." I decided that I didn't care if my boss was unhappy, if he fired me, then so be it. I didn't know it at the time, but I was purging myself of the dreaded and complex feelings dam. The feelings dam is quite simply where you make decisions based not on what needs to be done, but instead on what you think will make people feel better and be happy. When you decide to put a feelings dam in your life and get yourself entangled in all sorts of negative complications, your life starts to degrade. A feelings dam will pull you very powerfully into the disaster state. We may feel obligated as good people to weigh people's feelings over the business purpose. This never works. People, in the end, will respect what you and your company stand for. I made the decision that day to stand for something, and that immediately made my life much more meaningful. My first task was to become an expert in the design of experiments (DOEs) because it could efficiently solve process problems permanently.

I embarked on my first DOE to try to understand the screen print process and what could be done to eradicate the soldermask ink smear problem. Soldermask is that green coating you see on your computer's motherboard. Back in Photocircuits' day, a green soldermask image would be screen printed on the circuit board. This image could not be put on metal where it would be later solder coated, because without the solder, components could not be attached to the board. The precision with which the green coating had to be printed was sometimes as tight as six thousands of an inch: the thickness of two human hairs. The ink smear problem was simply the green ink smearing from the screen image during printing. Think of a t-shirt being screen-printed and seeing a fuzzy image. What causes that fuzzy image is ink smear. The print from my screens had to be very clean and very sharp.

One of the things I changed in the experiment was the type of soldermask ink. Sometimes I used the conventional ink that was made by a company owned by one of John Endee's close friends, and on other runs I used a different ink from Sun Chemical. The people at Sun explained how you want ink to flow in a screen print process. The science of how a complex fluid flows is called *rheology*. The people at Sun understood rheology. The current soldermask supplier did not understand the importance of rheology. What was found in the experiment was that if you choose the right type of squeegee and used the Sun Chemical ink, you would have dramatically less ink smear. The relationship between the variables—squeegee and ink—is known as an interaction. The result from using one ink versus another depends on the type of squeegee you use.

An example of an interaction might be if you had a mountain bike and a road bike. On a sunny, clear day you can go faster over a specified distance with the road bike. But on a rainy day, those thin tires will puncture on the slightest pebble you bike over. Eventually, you will be walking with the road bike. The mountain bike won't have flats. So the bike that will go fastest down the road—mountain or road bike—*depends* on whether it is sunny or rainy. People aren't very good at anticipating these dependencies or interactions. We have little intuition for it, but DOEs are extremely efficient at identifying the interactions.

Life was looking up until I had my meeting to review my test results and verifications for the new process using the new ink. John Endee was not happy with the test, or me, or anything that I did because he didn't like the answer I came up with. John had strong feelings for his friend at the current ink supplier and the thought of changing completely to Sun was repugnant to him. The feelings dam once again raised its very ugly head. Looking into John Endee's eyes, I thought I was going to be eaten alive. Rather than talk about the conclusions, he decided to dig into why I took so many measurements for each experimental run. I attempted to explain the statistics. He didn't care. He didn't want to change ink suppliers. He didn't like the fact that I took so much data because, in his opinion, I should have just known the answer if I was an engineer of any substance. Things did not go well in this meeting, and I finally blew my top and just walked out of it. Let me repeat, dam-thinking and flow-thinking cannot exist in the same space in harmony. There will be very nasty conflicts. A company has to choose one or the other, and there is only one right choice. Finding me on a bench in the parking lot, my boss sent me home. I turned on the TV and watched the Space Shuttle Challenger blow up. It was not a good day for me. I was very unhappy.

What I read in the paper and what I subsequently read in Richard P. Feynman's book on the space shuttle disaster created a strong connection for me with the engineers at Thiokol. The bottom line was that the NASA managers didn't want to listen to the engineers at Thiokol and their bad-decision making (where bad behavior and dam-thinking were at the root) created a disaster that needlessly killed people. I decided I would never work for a company like Photocircuits ever again. Still, I developed many professional connections at Photocircuits that accelerated my career. I will always be grateful for the experience. I learned a lot. It was a once-in-a-lifetime experience.

STORY POINT 5:
Letting Your Customers Set Your Standards is a Dangerous Game

And it is a game that always produces massive amounts of unhappiness. Back in the 1980's, many companies had the mantra that the customer was king. At this time, Toyota was putting severe stress on the Big Three automakers. Part of the mythology, amplified by the experts and the books written, was that Japanese companies had a culture of doing anything the customer wanted. Making the customer king was not something Toyota did, because that's just bad business. You can't let your customers set your standards. You can't allow your customer to dominate you. If you do, the end result will be destructive for both of you.

Over the years, I have become an advocate of sales processes taught by Miller Heiman and explained in books authored by Bill Stinnett, such as *Think Like Your Customer* and *Selling Results*. The first step in any decent sales process is to define your ideal customer. Without that you are flying blind and you will hit a mountain slope and wreck your company. In the Customer X radar chart that follows, we see some items such as *Growing* or *Trouble*. Growing and trouble are two out of the four modes a company can be in according to Heiman. The other two are overconfident and even keel. Essentially, if a company is growing or in trouble it is more likely to consider solutions from outside its existing supplier network. When the customer is content, you stand little chance of making a good case. Going quickly around the chart; *High End, High Profit* pertains to the customer's product positioning in their market—commodity or value. The more value oriented a customer was, the stronger my client's case could be made. Innovative: is the customer like Apple or like Walmart? My client felt where they provided value was through their speed and quality. They needed to work with companies that had a significant R&D budget and they needed access to engineers.

Customer X

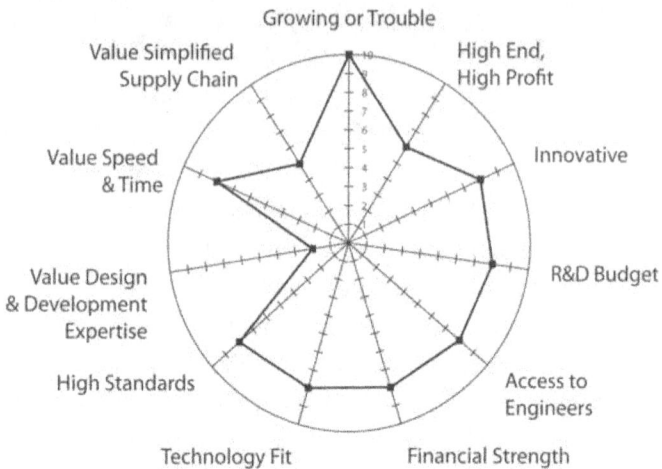

Figure 6: Evaluate Your Customers

I find that my clients like radar diagrams once they start actively using them for making decisions. You can see and compare a number of parameters all at once. You could also use different parameters than are shown here with Customer X. There is no one right way. For example, you could use the same radar diagram as Employee Y for evaluating Customer X! It is all up to you and what you need.

Often, companies block this access by making you deal with the buyer only. This wouldn't be acceptable for my client in the long run because the client had no ambition to produce low-cost, low-value, high-volume product. Financial strength is important, but might also provide an opportunity for my client to make the case that if the customer works with them, they will realize their financial goals sooner rather than later. Does the technology that my client provides enable what the customer wants? If it doesn't fit, is it worthwhile for my client to learn and expand the firm's technology in Customer X's direction? Does the customer hold himself to high standards and always strive to improve? Or do they allow their own customers to be pushy? My client had design and development capability. Did the customer value this? In the case of Customer X, they didn't value this, but this might have been because they didn't know much about it. If so, what would be the best way for Customer X to learn about my client's design and development (D&D) capability? My client wanted to produce product with very short lead times. Did this match customer X's needs? Did the customer want fewer suppliers and was that need a driving force for decisions? My client had strategies for customers to simplify the supply chain.

Customer X was a good fit. But my client had another customer who beat them up on price and wouldn't allow changes made to the materials selection and processing, which would greatly reduce manufacturing costs and improve yields. Based on evaluating this customer using the same parameters as customer X, my client decided that they wouldn't do business with customers who were a poor fit for them. Upon notifying this customer that, on a specific date, no more orders from them would be accepted, their tune changed. They allowed access to the engineers, they allowed for a conditional price increase until design changes and process changes required for a better more buildable part were put in place. Communication (almost overnight) moved from dealing directly with the buyer to many people at different levels communicating between my client and the customer. It went from a simple transactional relationship that was proving destructive, to a more complex, partnership relationship that possessed win-win opportunities.

It doesn't always work this way, but when you hold your company up to a high standard and are willing to walk away from the negotiating table, your customers will respect you. The start of any sales process is all about defining your standards and living up to those standards, even if the customer gets upset with you at times. In the end, everyone is much happier than if you tried to manage feelings and allow for a relationship of unequal footing.

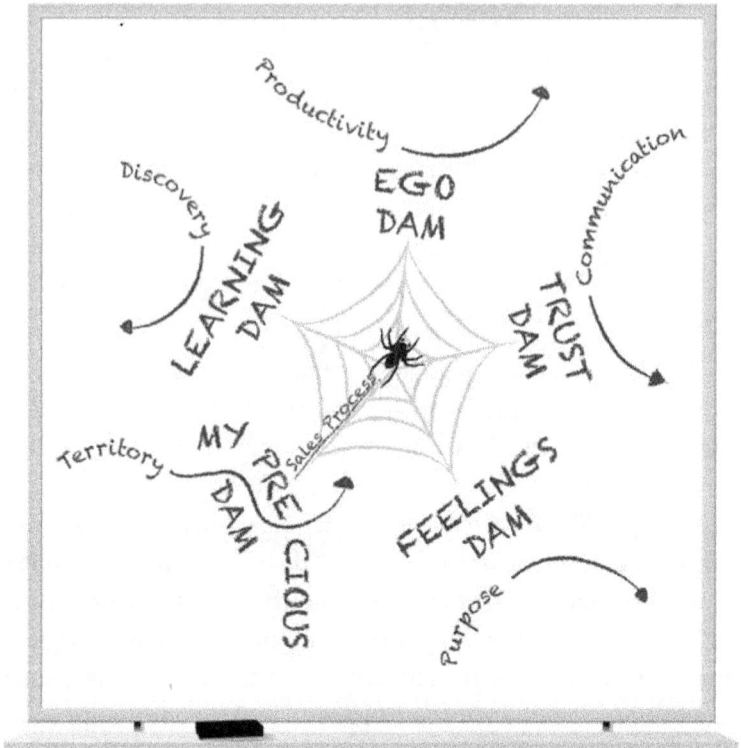

Figure 7: "Sales Process" Spider Diagram

We have used the web to describe how pulling strongly on one dam from the center of the web, will weaken and pull on all of the other dams. There is another way to think about this. If you discover that your sales force is very territorial, meaning that they have a *My Precious* dam, then you likely have all of the other dams too. People often defend a My Precious by manipulating people with their feelings, not asking for help, not communicating what they are doing outside their narrow silo, and being unwilling to have anyone learn anything about the customer. The existence of one dam implies the existence of all of the other ones too, because all of the dams aren't independent of each other—they are all connected to each other! The best and strongest way to pull down the My Precious dams in your company is by applying a complex sales process such as that recommended by Miller Heiman. If you want high profits, you want all of your relationships with all of your important customers to be complex. You do not want them complicated or transactional where your only point of contact is between your account manager and the customer buyer, even though you will be directed to do just that.

CHAPTER 5

*The Five Thinking Dams and
How They Stop Flow*

---

*We are continually faced with a series of
great opportunities brilliantly disguised as
insoluble problems.*

—John W. Gardner

If you go to Mesa Verde National Park, in the four corners region (Arizona, Utah, New Mexico, and Colorado), you will see the Anasazi cliff-dwelling settlements that mark the apex of the Anasazi civilization that flourished around AD 1200. Before the end of that century, around 1280, the Anasazi suddenly disappeared. Nobody knows what happened to them. This was a civilization whose roots predate the Romans (somewhere around 1000 B.C.). The Anasazi were known to build pueblo structures. They always choose settlements rather than living the nomadic life. Their hallmark was their cliff dwellings. Cliff Palace and

White House Ruins, for example, catch our eye. The structures emerge naturally out of the high cliff rock. Like the Roman road, the Appian Way, where you would see deep ruts carved by the wood wheels that transported people and goods, the steps leading up to these dwellings have deep indentations from feet rubbing off sandstone, bit by bit. People went up and down, thousands of times, continually following the same path. When I look at the dwellings, I have the impression of life patterns that repeat with little change.

We don't like change. We naturally gravitate toward ruts. After all, we have been trained in the ancient traditions and ways of dam-thinking. Ritual and repetition provide a sense of security for us. The problem is that a sense of security gets in the way of our ability to learn, change, and adapt. Following old patterns of thought is the hallmark of a dam-thinking culture. Dam-thinking prevents companies from growing fast, if at all. In order for your company to compete, you have to push against the dam-thinking wall. Your mission is to get rid of all dam-thinking in your company. It isn't an easy road and it isn't well traveled. You must accept the uncertainty, the perceived risk, and the anxiety, because this is the price you have to pay in order to achieve unlimited growth. Once people experience a flow culture and understand its power, they will be changed forever. They will never go back to the ancient cliff dwellings.

One of the keys to the success of Toyota has been their much lauded Toyota Production System. I learned the system at AlliedSignal when Larry Bossidy was CEO. Larry preached Six Sigma and Lean (a form of the Toyota Production System) both inside and outside of the company. Six Sigma and Lean spread to General Electric, because its CEO Jack Welch was a good friend of Larry Bossidy. Since then, many companies have had their own implementation experiences—both good and bad.

When I met the Toyota Production System expert assigned to our division and asked what the system was, he could not explain it to me. He just knew the implementation steps. He didn't understand how it all worked. He was climbing the steps to the Anasazi cliff dwelling and showing others how to climb the same exact steps. In essence, flow-thinking techniques were being taught within a dam-thinking format! What happens when you use flow-thinking tools with dam-thinking tactics? A mess. It starts with infighting and, left to grow on its own, it will turn your company to rubble. I have seen it too many times. An understanding of the five thinking dams will help you create the flow culture you need and get away from the cliff dwelling mentality that doom so many companies.

THE FIVE THINKING DAMS

The thinking dams have been introduced to you already in the previous chapters and story points. It is still worthwhile to collect them together so you can get your head wrapped around all of them. The five thinking dams are: ego, feelings, trust, My Precious, and learning. These dams stop the flow of productivity, purpose, communication, territory, and discovery. You know you are dammed when you see pressure, stagnation, or pollution. If they are there, and you deny it and think you have a flow-thinking culture, then your future becomes the disaster quadrant.

What follows is a very quick explanation of the thinking dams. The ego dam creates poor productivity because no one asks for help and people break rules meant to prevent accidents and disasters. The feelings dam erodes your business purpose because management sacrifices purpose in order to make people feel better. The trust dam stops communication because everyone is scared about what might happen to them if they speak out. The

My Precious dam restricts territory and creates deep silos because employees can't give up what they think they own, even though they don't own it—it belongs to the company. The learning dam stops all discoveries and, without new discoveries, your company can't grow. The following table summarizes how each dam stops an important flow.

Table 2: The Five Thinking Dams

The _____ Dam Stops	The Flow of _____
Ego	Productivity
Feelings	Purpose
Trust	Communication
My Precious	Territory
Learning	Discovery

THE EGO DAM STOPS THE FLOW OF PRODUCTIVITY

The ego dam grows if you hold back and don't ask for help. This means something that could be resolved sooner gets resolved later, if at all. This behavior blocks productivity. But the ego dam gets much worse when your people think the safety rules don't apply like the engineers at Chernobyl or the rules of law don't apply like our almost impeached president Richard Nixon. Not asking for help and breaking rules sets you up to be AIG like, Enron like, or BP like. The ego dam blocks productivity in a big way!

When I worked for AlliedSignal Laminate systems, we were a supplier to a number of very large factories. One of those factories was a large one located in Phoenix, Arizona. It went through a number of ownership changes such as Continental Circuits, which then became Hadco, and then Sanmina, and then Sanmina-SCI. Recently, I drove by the site and looked through the wire fence. This scene reminded me of the broken windows I saw driving on the Cross-Bronx Expressway as described in Chapter 4. The large Phoenix division of Sanmina-SCI, which had revenues at one time pushing $250 million per year, had been bulldozed to the ground. This Phoenix-based division didn't treat its suppliers very well.

I remember my first trip to Continental Circuits when I was working for Norplex/Oak (later to become AlliedSignal Laminate Systems). The people I was with at Norplex were all a bit tense during this visit. Walking into one of the many buildings on the campus, and then later walking through the facility, things were very disorganized, hectic, and tense. In the meetings that followed, there was no in-depth conversation about how to make Continental better. It was just a simple, matter-of-fact rattling off of all the things they felt we were doing wrong. I sensed apathy about us being their supplier. They just wanted to end the meeting and move on with the more important items scheduled for the rest of the day. They saw us as a burden. They did not understand that it was important to us that they did well. We were anything but apathetic. We were motivated to help if they asked. Like many companies, they were uneasy about their supplier being deeply involved in their process and working side by side with their people. Just like individual people that have life challenges, their ego was getting in the way of asking for help.

About ten years later, Mark Hollinger ran the facility in Phoenix. Today, he is the President of MacDermid Offshore Solutions. MacDermid has an oil exploration business, which Mark runs, and a specialty chemical business, with which I became familiar as far back as my experience with Beehive. Under

Mark's leadership, Continental Circuits started a very aggressive growth curve in which suppliers were brought in and worked with his people to improve his division in a very involved way. Suppliers and Mark's employees worked very closely together on a number of important initiatives.

One of the problems I worked on with Dan Buxton of Continental and Brad Jones of SAS was a particularly nasty problem called multilayer printed circuit board registration. What we did to dramatically improve the problem was create a flow of small, compact DOEs that challenged the basic assumptions people had about it in the industry. Prior to this work, registration was regarded as a material problem—specifically, a problem with the base fiber glass material. After this work, registration was regarded as a tooling and equipment problem with the alignment processes at the board fabrication level. The work produced a patent for AlliedSignal Laminate Systems, and the patent is now owned by Isola Laminate Systems. I, along with Rich Pangier, who oversaw the entire Continental account, and my boss at the time, Craig Cooley, won the AlliedSignal Premier Achievement Award for Customer Satisfaction. This was an award for which we competed with everyone in the entire corporation, across all three divisions. There were only two awards given out that year for customer satisfaction. I got to talk with Larry Bossidy back at the corporate facility in Morristown, and I received a modest stock award. We all had a nice dinner, and Larry gave his usual intense speech. Larry's speech was about the importance of the AlliedSignal name, which a few years later, ironically, he would give up in favor of Honeywell! Removing the ego dam and working with your suppliers and asking for help will improve your business significantly. After Mark left Continental, the old ego dams returned. I thought of all of it as I looked at the rubble that was once the original site of Continental Circuits.

THE FEELINGS DAM STOPS THE
FLOW OF PURPOSE

It's so hard for my clients to admit and deal directly with the feelings dam. It really gets back to the fact that no matter what you do or say, you will never make everyone happy. So why try? Focus on the purpose. If the purpose is a good one, you will find people that will help you and follow you. If you have a feelings dam, you will never ever be a good leader. For any leader, the feelings dam is out of control when poor performance and pollution are accepted, because people say they are working hard. The leader must keep the business focused on the performance and hold people accountable to the standard despite people's expressed negative feelings.

When I worked at Photocircuits, I specified and recommended an expensive piece of equipment based on a feelings dam. It all started with my boss returning from a trade show with a brochure explaining a piece of equipment with an unconventional design. The person who gave him the brochure was a friend of his. My boss seemed to be very enthusiastic about the whole situation and encouraged me to look at the equipment. I thought I would be a nice guy. I chose to overlook the real concerns I had about the design in favor of having my boss feel good and support his friend. This, in turn, made me feel good and comfortable. I was going with the flow (of feelings) instead of against the flow (of feelings) which might result in people being tense, nervous, or upset.

When the machine was delivered there were problems right from the get-go. Some old-timer maintenance people whispered in my ear, "Gray, get rid of this thing. We have seen this before. It will be bad for you." The machine had been wired completely backward. The ventilation system didn't work right. And after only a week of operation the machine became unsafe to operate. I spent months of wasted effort to try to make the machine work. I was determined not to fail. In the end it was a mess. The machine never did work right. I (and not my boss) was blamed for the fiasco, as I should have been. What is particularly bad when we allow feelings to override our otherwise good decision making is feelings provide an excuse for pollution: bad thinking, bad performance, and bad equipment. That event triggered me to look in the mirror and say, "Never again. I will never allow feelings to pollute my otherwise good decision making."

Flow cannot tolerate pollution of any kind, and when you let it in, removing pollution is very difficult. Inspection is a way to remove pollution, but it also represents a lack of trust in the production process. Have you ever wondered why inspectors and operators rarely talk to each other? It's the trust dam followed quickly by a My Precious dam between the inspectors and operators. Trying to fix the pollution created from a thinking dam, like the feelings dam, causes the other dams to pop-up. Over the long haul, dam-thinking tactics makes things worse.

Managers need to look for the feelings dam in their direct reports. If they see it, they need to encourage their employees to express their true thoughts. Employees need to understand that if they hold information back or communicate untrue information, because of feelings, that this is damaging to the purpose and the objectives of the company. This behavior can put the company into a an unrecoverable disaster scenario.

THE TRUST DAM STOPS THE
FLOW OF COMMUNICATION

Like the feelings dam, it's difficult for people to admit that the trust dam exists. We never want to tell someone we don't trust them, because if there *was* trust it will disappear. Trust is not something we want to lose with anyone. The only way trust can be repaired is with communication. With one of my clients, I saw trust dissolve within a whole division. A schism had developed that grew into a major fracture, because of the behavior of the responsible manager. Instead of encouraging communication between the two divided factions, he decided to be the mediator and discouraged direct communication. All communication had to run through him! At the same time he told both sides they were right in order to make both sides feel good! Things escalated out of control.

The problem that divided the people at this company was how to run experimental engineering product through the factory (which would provide new orders in the future) without slowing down the existing production orders that paid the bills. The experimental product would use production materials, production equipment, production operators, and could cause missed deliveries because of interruptions to production flow. Without the engineering work, there would be no experimentation, learnings, discoveries, or technological advancement. There would also be no new business because development work was required in order to land manufacturing contracts with products at the beginning of their growth curve. On one side, the engineers felt that all of the data entry and procedures slowed them down and consumed too much of their time. They had a point. On the opposite side, manufacturing needed information inserted into their system in order to manage the shops materials, deliveries, and costs. They had a point. The issues involved were complex and neither side would back down. The former manager overseeing these two groups tried to make both sides feel good as he told everyone what to do within his own My Precious management silo. This didn't work because nothing was resolved. What grew was an extreme lack of trust and (predictably) a breakdown in communication.

When I was called into this situation, people were unhappy and very unproductive. Getting them to talk was a real effort. One way I patched things up and started to build trust was by employing Edward De Bono's technique, the Six Thinking Hats, which is described in the book with the same name. What happens in many discussions concerning complex problems is that pointless, competitive arguments break out. I once saw a motivational speaker, explain this by holding up the front of a book saying, "what you see and I see are different, because you see the back side of the book and I see the front side of the book. The only way both of us can see the same thing is if both of us look at the same side of the book together." This is called parallel thinking.

With the Six Thinking Hats technique you do a parallel examination, which can be best through of as looking at three different books. You have the book that has a white hat on the front and a red hat on the back. The white hat is data and facts, and the red hat is feelings and emotions. You have another book that has a yellow hat on the front and a black hat on the back. The yellow hat is optimistic, all of the good things about an item, and the black hat is pessimistic, all of the bad things or risks associated with an item. Finally, you have a book that has a green hat on the front and a blue hat on the back. The green hat is for creative ideas and the blue hat is for the process that allows a team to move forward.

The team used a white hat, red hat, yellow hat, and black hat to understand and describe the current situation. Then this information was compiled into themes. After that, a green hat for ideas about how to make the situation better, and a blue hat for different implementation strategies, was used. Finally, by using the yellow and black hats, the scenarios were ranked and a decision was reached. Nobody was fighting, everyone was working productively, and a tremendous amount of work was done in two hours—more work than was achieved over the last six months with the trust dams and My Precious dams.

Debono's system allows for a complete improvisation of how to conduct parallel thinking sessions. What emerges from these sessions happens very quickly and is very creative, valuable, and surprising. The Debono system is much more about flow than the rigid Six Sigma value-mapping sessions that can become enormously complicated. For some business problems, I will blend elements of Six Thinking Hats with some of the more effective tools of Six Sigma. In order to maximize trust within a team, I allow everyone to be involved with me in the improvisation as we pick and choose together what we feel we need to use and what we need to do.

THE MY PRECIOUS DAM STOPS
THE FLOW OF TERRITORY

The *My Precious* dam comes from the story of *The Lord of the Rings*. The character Gollum pets and obsesses over the ring of power, repeating, "My Precious" over and over again. Gollum's health was affected very negatively by his need to possess the ring of power exclusively for himself. He became hideous and despicable. That is exactly what happens when people in a company think they own a product, process, invention, business unit, or factory and try to cling to what really wasn't theirs to begin with. It's a combination of irrational fears, silos, and intimidation tactics. A My Precious dam is very destructive for any company.

Many people I talk to initially get confused about how the My Precious dam blocks territory. Many people, when they see *territory,* think *territorial,* and that isn't what I mean at all. If you want to understand the true meaning of territory, think of what Lewis and Clark must have felt when they saw the vast expanse of the Great Plains for the first time. You want your people to see your company in exactly the same way: a massive territory where everyone can roam around—a possibility space, growth space, and contribution space without limits. Now imagine this same territory cut to pieces with grain silos and barbed wire fences. It now becomes very tricky in terms of where you can and can't go. Even worse, it's dynamic because fences and silos change, move, and grow. From day to day, you don't know where you can and can't go. Soon, you too put up your own fence and silo so that you at least preserve your job—preserve your ever diminishing territory!

I had a client company in which management wasn't happy with their engineering investment. The engineers were very territorial, clinging to their narrow avenues of expertise. Customers started to get frustrated, because they needed this small (but significant) technology company to be improving and accelerating. The engineering silos were preventing them from masterminding together, experimenting together, learning together, and coming up with the novel discoveries required to keep the company valuable.

The first step to break down the silos was to form SCRUM teams around the engineers. (See Story Point 8 on page 133 for a description of SCRUM.) To start, all of the engineers were gathered together and they made a list of all of their tasks, projects, and responsibilities. Management determined the priority of the tasks. This prioritized list became the master backlog. The second step was to create a subset of items from the master backlog that would become their first sprint backlog. The engineers decided how many of the high priority items could be completed in 30 days.

At first, the amount of items that the team could complete within the short 30 day time box for the first sprint was almost nil. There were two reasons for this: one, the engineers thought of themselves as specialists and no engineer could venture onto another's territory—a My Precious dam—and, two, the constant problems on the floor demanded each engineer's individual area of specialized expertise. It looked like the effort to create a SCRUM team would fail. The My Precious dam was removed with a *simple complex solution,* which changed the individual dynamic into a team dynamic, instantly. The urgent factory work became the responsibility of the team and not the individual expert! The SCRUM team had already been made responsible for the projects. The team had also been made accountable for results. In order to get the firefight work done, two-man teams would serve a two-week rotation to handle all of the issues on the floor. If they had time, they could continue work on the SCRUM team projects. At first, this met with resistance. One complaint was that engineers who didn't know a process couldn't solve a problem. Management then raised the standard. Every engineer possessed basic problem-solving skills. Every engineer was expected to learn all of the process areas. What better way to learn and discover than by working on real problems? You know you are in flow when you sense that you are behind and there is no time to procrastinate. You simply have to start taking action and do high-value activities that move the pojects and solve problems. Once a day, for one hour in the afternoon, the engineers could come together as a team to discuss all of the factory firefight issues.

Complex solutions are always massively parallel. Engineers became more interested in their work and started to experiment and discover new things on processes with which they were unfamiliar. Operators wouldn't ask for help from firefighters who didn't understand their area, so they started solving their own problems by themselves and taking accountability for their work areas. Engineers began to see the dependencies between all of the processes and this changed the nature of their project work. Finally, engineers discovered very quickly the advantages of working together rather than alone. They started to mastermind and come up with solutions that couldn't be derived by themselves. The My Precious dam at this client's firm had been dissolved quickly just by changing a few rules, changing a few standards, and making a team accountable for results so that every individual was responsible for the results of the team. Consequently, the engineers were happier, more energized, and looked forward to the start of their day.

THE LEARNING DAM STOPS THE FLOW OF DISCOVERY

When I rejoined AlliedSignal Laminate Systems, I decided to go after the holy grail of printed circuit board fabrication—multilayer printed circuit board registration. This was a problem, that saw almost no progress for almost two decades in this industry. Why? Because, everyone in the entire industry were convinced they thought they knew what the problem was, yet everyone had a different belief. There was constant debate and friction and fear generated by people holding fast to their differing ideology. At times it looked like a war. Very few people were open minded enough to reject what they thought in order to create a common ground of understanding based on data and real discovery using design of experiments. The entire industry suffered from a learning dam.

If you open the box to your computer and pull out your motherboard, you will see the green soldermask all over its surface, dotted with small and large black squares and rectangles. The largest black square is typically the brain—the mighty processor. As processors have grown in power, the number of connections required has grown and the amount of space required to make those connections has shrunk. Making all of the connections has necessitated constructing skyscrapers of connections within the thickness of the printed circuit board!

Think of the printed circuit board as a flattened out spinal column. A flattened out spinal column would have nerves running through its entire thickness. The printed circuit board is the same way. It has wire-like conductors running all through its thickness. In order to understand the difficulties of making such a thing (in which everything is properly connected) think of a sandwich. A sandwich for a printed circuit board starts with a very thin piece of fiberglass. It may be as thin as two thousandths of an inch (a little less than the thickness of a human hair) to as thick as 14 thousandths of an inch (a little less than the thickness of five human hairs). If you were to look at the surface of your sandwich piece, it would look very geometric, with very thin copper conductors running all over the surface on both the top side and the bottom side. What you have at this point is one sandwich slice. Up to nine sandwich slices may be required in order to make all of the required connections. How do you stick all of these layers together? You put bonding material in between each sandwich piece. Think of the bonding material as glue. You put the entire sandwich in a lamination press, under high heat and high pressure, in order to completely glue everything together.

What registration means is that you put something where it was intended and everything lines up. On a printed circuit board, tens of thousands of small things have to line up to a very high level of precision. Consider a color magazine that has to print multiple layers of colors, one on top of the other, in order to create the full color gamut. When a print of one color fails to line up with the previous print of the other color, then the print has misregistered. The printer has a registration problem, and when it happens from time to time it is very obvious. Occasionally, you will see this on a few pages of a magazine.

What has to be lined up in a printed circuit board are all of the internal conductor images, and all these have to line up with the drill that makes all of the holes. How many holes? Sometimes upwards of 40,000 to 80,000. The diameter? Sometimes smaller than six thousandths of an inch in diameter, or two human hairs! One miss—or sometimes even a partial miss—will result in a defective board. What makes things really difficult is the fact that your individual sandwich slices move when you laminate them together. And each sandwich slice layer moves differently!

My problem, the printed circuit board registration problem, can best be understood if you think of an archer standing 50 feet away from a target. The archer has to hit the bull's-eye to within five thousandths of an inch and do this 40,000 times. What makes this particularly difficult is that the targets will move after you fire off your arrow! My job was to figure out how to predict where the target would be after firing off an arrow. The task before me was daunting. Pretending that I could get anywhere with it on my own looked like madness to my coworkers.

I remember my boss at the time, Craig Cooley. He yelled at me, his veins popping out of his neck, asking me who I thought I was! How arrogant could I be! Things like that. I just looked at him until he was exhausted and said, "Do you want to fire me?" I had become a manager's worst nightmare. In all fairness to Craig, he learned to adapt, and we both became friends who have a lot of respect for each other. Anyway, after my comments, Craig got his second wind and went on about all the PhDs that had worked on the problem (for decades apparently) down at UOP (which today is a Honeywell Company) in Des Plaines, Illinois. When he said that, I had a slight flashback.

I remembered Bill Rowsell showing me a piece of printed circuit laminate with a watermark on it when he took me on my first tour of Beehive Circuits. The watermark contained the letters *UOP.* UOP was the original company that bought and grew Norplex into one of the first PCB laminate suppliers, which later became AlliedSignal Laminate systems. He waved that laminate in front of me and explained that I would never get bored in this industry. I later looked up UOP because I wanted to know who they were and what the company did. UOP is the Bell Laboratories, the NASA, of catalytic cracking. Their services, designs, and processes are used in refineries all over the world. The point is that the folks at UOP are really smart! When you have really smart people collected closely together in one place, it is really hard to keep them contained without them creating something that departs from the primary business. I saw this happen firsthand when I worked at Monsanto. It is no surprise that, one day long ago, somebody over at UOP decided to buy Norplex.

When the multilayer registration project was assigned to me (because nobody wanted to fire me) I got a call from UOP headquarters in Des Plaines, Illinois. The fellow on the other end of the line wanted to know if I wanted all of the files concerning their work on multilayer printed circuit board registration. I asked, "Well, how much stuff do you have?" And he came back with, "Files upon files; literally a truckload of paper." I thought to myself, "These guys are so smart, I wouldn't even begin to understand what they were doing." I had a flashback of Matt Tirrell and the chalk dust flying everywhere.

I shook a little, wiped the sweat off my brow, and considered the madness of looking at all of that paper. What I did know was that they were trying to find the perfect analytic solution at UOP. I knew from my factory floor experience with design of experiments and other empirical approaches that I could solve problems without really understanding what I was doing. After a pause I said, "No, thank you. Keep it." There was stunned silence on the other end. I know they were insulted, but I couldn't help how they felt. They had been working on the project for some 15 years with minimal progress. I knew there wasn't going to be much I could learn within the artificial environment of a laboratory such as the one at UOP. I needed to have my work contained within the real production flow of the factory. Only that information was relevant to me, and there wasn't much of it at the start.

The first person I called was Brad Jones at SAS Institute. Later, others from both Continental Circuits and AlliedSignal became involved. We all did great work over a period of almost eight months. Often, we worked the graveyard shifts as we bartered for production time. Once, I was cornered by an irate production manager who couldn't understand how I got so many panels through his process in such a short period of time. His jobs were running late and mine were early. I had spent considerable time with the operators on the off-shifts. I would just stand there in a corner, quietly watching and observing my panels. Eventually, people would come up to me. Over time, as they noticed my pattern, more people would want to talk to me. I explained what I was doing. And I clowned around with some of them, too. What happened as a result of my socialization with them was that when they saw my panels, they blasted them through the process.

The reason why the project was successful was that all assumptions and previous beliefs were challenged. Articles from Bell Laboratories claimed that the bonding material used to glue all of the layers together had nothing to do with movement. What I found strange was the lack of data in those papers. It was all based on assumptions and theories as far as I could discern. The papers I authored explained everything done, showed the data, and the statistical analysis. The data proved the Bell articles were wrong. The bonding-sheet type, the orientation of the bonding sheet (width and length), and the amount of glue they contained (resin) strongly affected the movement of the thin circuit sandwich slices. There were other assumptions, too, that were proven wrong. For example, it was assumed that if you had material that didn't move you wouldn't have a registration problem. Wrong! We found out that the primary source of the registration problem was not the material, but the printed circuit board fabrication process— specifically, issues related to tooling, such as artwork, alignment pins, the precision of punching alignment holes in panels, and so on. In fact, a non-expert would assume tooling would be more important than material shrinkage and growth. And the non-expert would be right! At times, as you become more expert, you develop blind spots for looking at the obvious. Finally, everyone on the team took notes, listened, and observed everything. This—more than the discoveries within the actual experimental data—proved to have the most immediate impact.

Once when we were at the plant, an older engineer got in my face and said to me, "You guys over there at Allied don't know what you are doing. You are costing us money. Every October something happens in your factory that causes all of our registration to go bad. This produces a ton of scrap for electrical shorts and electrical opens. Get your act together because the problem isn't with us, it is with you!" Wow. What a nice guy. Very open-minded, too. What he was describing became known as the October Surprise. Back at Allied, everyone cringed with fear, because everyone knew what was coming. When October came around again, it was bad.

There was so much scrap that all of Sanmina–Phoenix (which use to be Continental Circuits) was shut down. The core team and the extended team were called into action.

Standing in the middle of this mess, I felt strangely empowered. The team knew the process, every single, little detail, really well. Goodness knows how many panels we all watched collectively from beginning to end. I wondered if this is what my grandfather felt when he had a team of people, the schoolteachers, that always made careful observations about his factories and knew exactly where to look when a problem broke out. We knew there were only a few places to look for trouble, and one of those places was the artwork accuracy. For example, for each experimental run, we had to measure the artwork so that we could accurately compute the movement. About every fourth or fifth time, the artwork dimensions had changed and were off from what was thought.

So, when the team arrived to try to solve the mystery of the October Surprise, some people measured the artwork, while other people looked at other tooling issues. The team found that the artwork was way off from what it should have been. When the room temperature and humidity graphs where the artwork was used (called the print room) were looked at, they had gone way out of specification. The artwork material would move and change its dimensions if there was even a slight change in temperature and humidity. Every October we found a huge change in the temperature and humidity of the print room. This was the true source of the October Surprise. The problem was within the plant and not with the supplier. And our customer hadn't placed much value in observation, because this had been going on for years!

Listening and observing are so important and valuable, yet few people in business take much time doing these things. If you are going to be a flow-thinker, you will have to master these listening and observational skills. That is why I devoted Chapter 8 to these subjects.

STORY POINT 6:
Be on Time!

The biggest barrier to achieving accountability is the feelings dam. Let's say you want to hold people accountable to meet their commitments on time with no exceptions. What you are really saying is that you are serious about the purpose of your business to deliver a product on time. What is the important word here? *Time.* Time is money! If you go to Switzerland, what do you see? Clocks and watches of incredible precision. Is it any wonder that the country with the most lucrative banks, with a huge accumulation of wealth, has an obsession with time? Yet, when I walk around companies with their mission statements and values hanging on the walls, which are often very abstract to me, I not only fail to see anything concrete or important, such as references to accountability, but I also don't see the most basic and universally important concrete reference to being on time with everything! Why wouldn't a company, besides Federal Express, say that? Don't all companies essentially deliver a product? But it's worse than just a lack of a reference to time—many companies seem to be living in a world where time isn't important! And if time isn't important at your company, I suspect money isn't important either. When I look at all the clocks in a company I am visiting, they may be as much as 14 minutes apart! Contrast this with a typical European city, with big clocks all over the place, all going off at precisely the right time. Great cities like Venice, for example, have great clocks and they were the centers of great economic wealth. Their precision of time drove their economic engine. Has this law of the importance of being on time changed? Could you compete better globally by simply managing your time better and making your company operate like a Swiss watch?

Why is there a lack of accountability with time in so many companies? It is the feelings dam. In so many companies, there is often very little consequence if work is done late. An employee is allowed to complain that they are overworked and unhappy, that a supplier didn't have the right information, that management didn't give them the right instructions. Excuse after excuse, and all of the excuses are accepted. Why? Because management would rather accept the excuse than hurt the employee's feelings and say he or she is doing a terrible job. The business purpose rapidly erodes as importance is placed on feelings and not time.

Peer pressure is a wonderful thing. When you make a team accountable for getting things done on time, as with a SCRUM team, you immediately have complete transparency for the on time performance for everyone on the team. When the sprint starts, each person must report on his or her work each day. Quickly, everyone can see if the team is lagging or ahead. A quick scan of what has been completed on the sprint backlog will reveal who is lagging. A good team will fix the problem by itself.

It is amazing how differently everything will work when everyone expects everything to be on time.

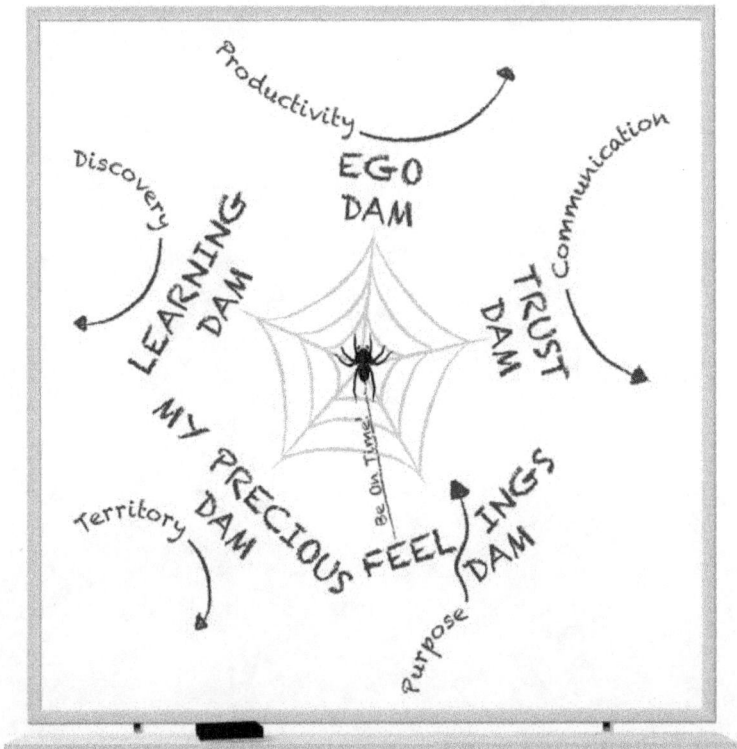

Figure 8: "Be On Time" Spider Diagram

Few things pull as powerfully against the feelings dam as having a team with an absolute expectation that everything must be done on time. SCRUM is all about time and meeting time commitments. SCRUM is also about teams. And a team that is slipping will use peer pressure to get other members of the team to conform. Being on time is also aligned with meeting our commitments and being accountable. Meeting commitments was a complex solution Steve Hochhauser used to transform the culture of AlliedSignal Laminate Systems, as described in Chapter 10.

CHAPTER 6

Scale-Up Insanity

Anything you build on a large scale or with intense passion invites chaos.

—Francis Ford Coppola

What kind of business can you build with burgers? In the fiscal year ending in 2008, McDonalds had over $23 billion in sales with an operating profit of $6.4 billion. It has 31,900 fast food operations in over 100 countries that employ 400,000 people. The burger business was never supposed to be this big. What was it that caused McDonalds to grow and dominate their market? Velocity. You do not have to wait. The amount of time from placing your order to getting your order is typically less than a minute. Quality. You know what everything should and will taste like. Emergence. How you get your order and who is involved are always different. The workers perform in what appears to be a loose and improvised manner. But if you look closely, everyone is communicating and checking one another. Just because what they are doing is improvised, it does not mean their activity is loose or undisciplined.

Scale is very important to any flow business, and McDonalds is very sensitive to scale. Look at the building footprint: compute the square feet and you will see it's very small. Remember W. L. Gore and the rule of 150. At McDonalds, there are very rarely more than seven people working. If you look at the production floor where the burgers are made, you will see a U-shaped arrangement of right-sized equipment that includes the cash register. Work cells promote efficiency, teamwork, and communication. Everything is scaled to a flow. All of the equipment is surprisingly small. If you had to, you could, essentially, put a McDonalds in a small closet! McDonalds thinks of small operations, but big business. So many companies think of themselves in terms of very large operations and usually wind up watching their profitability evaporate.

DAM-THINKERS AND FLOW-THINKERS AT MONSANTO

It was early April 1982, in Sauget, Illinois, an industrial town across the Mississippi river from St. Louis. I was standing at the top of a metal grating looking out over the W. G. Krummrich plant owned by Monsanto. The dream companies that a chemical engineering graduate wanted to work for back in the 1980's were Exxon, Procter & Gamble, DuPont, and Monsanto. I was listening to a business development manager. He said wispily that Monsanto tried to get into the detergent business, but found it couldn't compete with Procter & Gamble. He continued by saying that Monsanto would never again try such a foolish venture. I really thought that was an odd thing to say. I immediately wondered why? Why couldn't Monsanto compete with the great Procter & Gamble? I concluded that maybe I was naive and ignorant. Only years later did I return to this question with the intent of finding the answer.

As I would come to learn, this throwing in the towel on new business ventures, or selling businesses that were not tightly woven into their core competencies of fibers, chemicals, pharmaceuticals, and agriculture, was a repeating pattern—a very nasty habit— imbedded in the culture. If they wanted a new business, such as pharmaceutical drugs, they would just go out and buy a giant instead of starting one on their own. So, in 1985, at a cost of about $2.7 billion dollars, Monsanto bought G. D. Searle & Company. Overnight, Monsanto had become a pharmaceutical giant with product brand names such as Metamucil, Dramamine, Celebrex, Ambien, and NutraSweet. As significant as this acquisition was for Monsanto, it paled to what it could have had if it allowed business ideas to emerge fully and flourish with its own people working imaginatively in their vast array of buildings.

Monsanto had so many smart people inventing and creating new business ideas that if management had just listened they could have been the largest corporate entity in the world. Starting in the 1980's, deal making was the thing. Why build a business when you have heavy incentives to just buy or merge. This behavior (buying and becoming big) was over-rewarded and the promises made about the performance of the combined entity rarely materialized. Why? Few people understand that bringing two companies together is complex. Most merging companies create layers of infinite detail and complications that ignore the importance of people and culture. Furthermore, with many of these mergers, there was no sensitivity to scale. Create one giant enterprise and slap one name on it and you create a really big mess that will, in the end, blow itself apart. The bigger the business enterprise, the more unstable it becomes. By being and thinking that bigger was better in the banking business, we almost turned the entire US economy into an empty shell, like the cliff dwellings of the ancient Anasazi! And that threat still continues today! "Too big to fail," is an oxymoron!

To give an example of the huge potential inside Monsanto consider Monsanto Electronic Materials Company (MEMC), which goes by the trade symbol WFR today. This was a company that started out very small and was partly in the agricultural group and partly in the chemical group at Monsanto. In the beginning, some very clever people working in a Monsanto laboratory came up with a process for making ultrapure silicon in the late 1950's. This material, of course, became essential for semiconductor manufacturing. The timing for MEMC could not have been better. MEMC started as a very small business group just outside of St. Charles, Missouri. It was thought of as a niche business and not something that would rival the mighty chemical and agricultural group. But it grew in the 1970's and 1980's, and it was sucking up more resources and people and competing for budgets in a volatile business market. The rate of technology obsolescence, the amount of new capital that needed to be injected in order to play the game, the whole notion of unpredictable demand, just went against the staid cash cow businesses Monsanto was known for. As MEMC started to grow like a weed, Monsanto was faced with a really difficult decision. Keep it or sell it? MEMC was sold in 1989 to the European company Hüls AG. Today, MEMC is a highly respected $2 billion dollar company.

The problem Monsanto had was sitting right in front of me that day in 1982 as I stood in the sun on that metal grating platform. Everything was big at the W. G. Krummrich plant. Many pieces of equipment and technology were old. The products coming out of the plant, like sulfuric acid, were unexciting and predictable. The plant was a cash cow. And this was a small plant! Monsanto had plants many times this size.

Krummrich was a training ground for young, fresh engineers straight out of college to learn all about Monsanto's dam-thinking ways. Monsanto's dam-thinking culture was eroding. There was a price to be paid for hiring the best of the best. In the years that I worked there, I came to learn that the dam-thinkers and the flow-thinkers did battle each and every day.

APM—MONSANTO'S ADVANCED PERFORMANCE MATERIALS GROUP

I wasn't offered a job at the Krummrich plant back in 1982. The first person who interviewed me was from Cornell, and he made it known to me that he was Ivy League right from the start. He had me sitting quite far away from him, and I got the sense, just as I was to experience with the plant manager at Beehive Circuits, that he didn't like people. This was the only interview I ever had in my whole life where I was sitting down and the person talking to me was standing up! "So, Mr. McQuarrie, why are your grades so terrible!" I paused and thought, *"Because you're wrong and my grades aren't terrible,"* but they certainly weren't perfect. In my naiveté as a 17-year-old teenager, I tried to apply to Dartmouth and Harvard, and they informed me that I needed to be perfect—and I was far from perfect. When they told me that, I remembered how my grandfather explained how the Harvard MBAs at a large east coast consulting company couldn't figure out his production control system at Green Giant. Apparently, this management consulting firm failed to appreciate the power of the complex social network my grandfather created as they tried to implement a computerized production-control system. And my grandfather told me many times that he wasn't perfect and he didn't have a college degree. So I looked at this gentleman and knew I was going to have a tough time answering his question. I felt like the robot played by Arnold Schwarzenegger in the movie *The Terminator* considering various responses and choosing one from the list. I choose to argue! And I wasn't offered a job! And I thought it was just like the girl I was infatuated with in junior high school: that I would never see her or Monsanto in my life ever again. I was so wrong.

When I was working at Shipley in the spring of 1994, a good friend, who was a headhunter, called. He told me that there was a very important company that wanted someone with my experience: plating, process development, and design of experiments. A few weeks later I had dinner with Martin Rapp in Newton, Massachusetts. Marty Rapp was a young engineering manager at Monsanto who later became my boss. He was very much on a fast track at Monsanto. He was one of their best. At dinner I just looked at Marty. I could tell they had some sort of problem that needed sorting out fast. I was very nervous, because I just couldn't believe Monsanto thought I could help. As I would come to learn, Marty was very focused, high energy, and intense—a tall, lanky blond guy who took everything you said to him seriously. I never really saw Marty roll over laughing, but people with Marty's traits are always successful in business. We didn't always get along, but I always respected him, his directness, and what he stood for. Marty was completely devoid of any feelings dam. He did care, he did have feelings, but he also knew how to make some really tough decisions.

Marty liked what he heard at dinner and had me invited for in-depth interviews at Monsanto's corporate Creve Couer, Missouri, campus! At first I couldn't believe it. Monsanto wanted a guy who they rejected back in 1982 because his grades were no good? Later, I began to give myself more credit. Monsanto needed someone who could solve real world problems—and I had become recognized for that skill.

One of the first things Monsanto asked for before I went down there were my college transcripts. Why?! Not only that, they had to be official—not simple copies. Finally, everything was in order and I took off for St. Louis. When I landed, I was greeted by my guide, a PhD chemist who took me out to a great dinner and drove me around the expansive Creve Couer campus—it was huge. It looked like one of Cecil B. DeMille's epic movie sets where you could imagine the royal procession with trumpets and chariots. The CEO at that time, Richard Mahoney, worked in the secluded Building E. Dividing this campus was a freeway. On the east side were the scientists and engineers, and on the west side were the business people. A white shirt, black slacks, a modest tie, and well-polished shoes were appropriate attire for the east side. A very expensive business suit was appropriate for the west side. You could read Monsanto's culture by studying their corporate campus, just as an archeologist could read Roman culture by studying the Roman Forum. The buildings and campus spoke, and it was loud and clear: dam-thinkers do well at Monsanto.

The interview was extremely strange. I thought I was talking to two different companies with two different ways of thinking. And that was exactly what was going on. The first group had me sit at a table with five people asking me questions. This was known as a panel interview and, apparently, the APM group had invented a way to improve interview screening with their version of a panel interview. I can't remember the exact questions, but they were long questions and went something like this, "At APM we value an employee that can create change without making anyone upset, without creating any anxiety, and without creating any conflict. Please give us specific examples where you accomplished this." I was at a total loss. I tried to make up an answer only to be told my answer wasn't specific enough. Finally, I was allowed to ask a question. I asked, "What, generally, was the business plan for APM?" They said that the group only had about $3,000,000 in sales, but in five years or less they would be at $500,000,000 in revenue and the sky would be the limit. This was a little bit disconcerting considering the fact that they had real difficulty explaining to me what their products were and why anyone would want them and buy them. I was concerned. If this hadn't been Monsanto, I would have walked out the door right then and there because I was sensing a Beehive experience on a much grander scale.

After the panel interview, I was interviewed by Marty Rapp's boss, Dr. Frank Delk. Frank, as I was to learn, also went to Cornell. We became close friends over the years. Frank fundamentally changed the direction my career was to take. He turned me onto the fact that if I was going to solve real business problems, I needed to understand people and their behaviors. Frank remains a close friend and mentor. It was a very important day for me when I stepped into Frank's office and sat down comfortably against the right side of his desk. He must have been about two or three feet from me. I thought I was talking to a friendly student advisor back in my days at the University of Minnesota. He had a warm grin on his face and seemed to like people. It was as if he was expecting me, was glad I was there, and was excited to ask me some questions. I felt very much myself and I felt energized. The first question he asked went something like this, "Gray, over there on top of some papers are your college transcripts. I haven't looked at them. If I were to look at them, I want you to tell me in at most two words what they would say to me?" What a question! I paused for about a second. Looked into his eyes and said simply—"persistence!" I was hired! As I was to find out, Frank was a flow-thinker. I was a flow-thinker. Others in the group were dam-thinkers. I was about to experience part of a finger of a fissure that was splitting Monsanto into pieces. Dam-thinkers and flow-thinkers cannot exist in equilibrium. If you try to keep them together you will have a company that will tear itself apart from the inside.

THE SCALE-UP INSANITY

One of the primary products APM was actually selling was called Flectron®. Flectron was a polyester fabric (woven or nonwoven) that was plated with electroless copper or the combination of electroless copper and electroless nickel. What electroless means is that the plating happens without current. In order to understand electroless plating, let's start with a description of plating with current. If you remember high school chemistry, you might recall taking a bar of copper and dissolving it in sulfuric acid and a little bleach (hydrogen peroxide) or simply dissolving copper sulfate crystals in sulfuric acid. Then you took a brass plate, put it into the solution, and connected it to a battery (the details aren't important) so current can flow and presto—the dissolved copper in the beaker plates to the brass. To do the plating without current (electroless) you put an organic compound in this solution, such as formaldehyde, which breaks down rapidly. While breaking down, it surrenders electrons to the copper in the solution, turning the dissolved copper into copper metal. In order to make Flectron, the copper plating should appear only on the surface and not spontaneously plate all over the place in the bath, which is a very bad thing to have happen. Having plating happen on a metal surface or treated surface is a trick—a very important trick used in all sorts of applications from bumpers to the most sophisticated electronic devices. A trick that Photocircuits and Shipley spent a decade or more trying to sue each other over for patent infringement.

As you might imagine, the chemical bath required to pull this off was delicate and very sensitive to scale. The largest electroless copper bath I had seen was maybe 400 gallons. On my first day on the job at the APM Earth City site, I was standing on a metal grating, having flashbacks to my visit 12 years before when I was at the W. G. Krummrich plant. I couldn't believe my eyes. I was looking down at what must have been 6,000 gallons of electroless copper solution. It was an awesome site; audacious in every way. The whole production line, of which the tank was just one part, was in a huge, open hangar-like space, with a ceiling 30 or more feet high. Piled high, not too far from this tank, all the way to the rafters, were steel-reinforced, multi-hundred gallon containers of electroless copper solution. And we needed all of this chemistry because the bath would fall apart every other day! I thought to myself, how can anyone make money like this? And the answer was that we weren't making money. We were burning cash at a level that had gotten the executive management in E building excited. The clock was ticking, and APM was desperate for help. I could not believe what I had walked into. I wasn't sure where to begin. And where I began was a mistake, but a great learning lesson.

In order to discover how to get significantly more life out of the 6,000 gallon tank, I started plating on the adjacent pilot line that had a 40-gallon tank. Because MacDermid was the current supplier, they had become the designated bad guy. The MacDermid chemistry used was what we called a first generation bath, and some of the ingredients, such as cyanide, were difficult to deal with from a waste treatment perspective. This chemistry represented what was used in the very early days, the 1960's. The Shipley chemistry was a fifth generation bath that had a very sophisticated recipe of ingredients and was designed to plate very fast on printed circuit boards but had never been tried on a product like Flectron, which was very different than a printed circuit board. One of the first things I did was to call MacDermid and tell them, "We are going to use the Shipley chemistry, but please don't go away because what I am about to embark on may not work and I may need your help." My rule of always treating your suppliers well was put into motion.

After a little tank redesign with the small tank, we started plating with the Shipley chemistry. The plated copper quality was rough, grainy, splotchy, and dark—not the bright salmon pink color required for Flectron. We did a number of DOEs, and I was losing my confidence because nothing worked. According to the experts, we were looking at all of the right things that would affect the quality of the plating. There were lots of ingredients in this blue bath of stuff. Critical to it was some little organic stuff called the primary stabilizer. This stuff was like Tabasco sauce—you only needed a little bit because a little went a long way. This secret sauce was why the entire bath worked without it falling apart. Shipley adamantly asserted the primary stabilizer was not important; moreover, you couldn't measure it anyway, so you would have no way to adjust its concentration. Or so they thought!

On my fourth DOE, with no progress having been made, I decided to go out with my Shipley friends and enjoy a two-hour lunch. I told the operators not to do anything, not to adjust or make chemical additions to the bath; I told them to just leave it alone, but continue to plate. As a result of my command the primary stabilizer would slowly burn down and as a result change the characteristics of the plating. When we returned, there, coming out of the bath, was a beautiful salmon-colored copper deposit on the fabric. It was perfect! After deconstructing how the chemistries had been consumed, it became obvious that the ingredient that the experts thought wasn't important was the most important thing. The reduction in the concentration of primary stabilizer was absolutely critical. This wasn't the first time this happened to me, nor was it the last. It is the reason that when people say, "Gray, whatever it is, it isn't this!" that is the first place I look. I figured out how to burn down the stabilizer, initiate the correct plating structure, and adjust the chemical additions so that you would have perfect product using the Shipley chemistry coming out of the 40-gallon pilot line. According to my Monsanto friends, scaling up to the 6,000-gallon tank would be a breeze. It wasn't. I was about to learn the painful lesson that complex things just don't scale up well.

Where I had free reign over the pilot line, there was a whole team responsible for the large production line—and it needed a large team! The full production line was a very complicated, highly automated, extremely expensive beast. A beast that was about to eat me up for dinner and then spit me out. While the pilot studies were going on, a new 6,000-gallon tank was being built, based largely on Shipley's expert recommendations. With the plating perfected on the 40-gallon plating line, and the new 6,000-gallon tank ready to go on the full-scale production line, it was time for startup! Everyone waited with great anticipation. The general manger, my boss Marty, and everyone involved in this business unit was there to watch and celebrate. The startup process, the breaking in of the new bath, was initiated. Then came the real plating run. The very wide fabric started to exit the tank looking shiny and pink. And it really looked pink. Way too pink! I was thinking, "Oh my, this is really bad." After only five feet of fabric left the tank—disaster! Rollers shook and loud, screeching gears whaled. Operators yelled, "Stop everything!" The entire tank was plating out. The 6,000 gallons of chemistry had completely gone unstable. It was a mess. The general manger looked at me for about a minute without saying a word. Then he walked off back to his office. What was wrong? For any complex system, when you change the scale, you change everything. Despite perfecting the plating process on the 40-gallon plating line, I had learned absolutely nothing about plating on the 6,000-gallon plating line. When the old technology, first generation, MacDermid chemistry was run with the new tank configuration (which was very stable, because of the cyanide) fabric could be plated quickly with good mechanical and visual quality. And the bath rarely went unstable and crashed. Monsanto had its full production line working. But did they need it?

The original business plan was to use the large pieces of copper fabric to insulate walls of hospitals from electronic interference. Somehow someone got the notion that all hospital rooms throughout the world needed electronic shielding. When you have a dam-thinking culture with My Precious dams, which have deep silos, it is very easy for one person to lead a company very far astray and do really stupid things that create tremendous amounts of financial damage. So based on one or two people—who would have likely been fired in a flow-thinking culture based on their evaluations—all of the equipment and materials were scaled to meet this projected demand. Furthermore, the large scale of everything made the business look Monsanto-like, Krummrich-like. The assumption that justified the huge 6,000-gallon tank just wasn't real—hospitals were not interested in Flectron. What APM did find was that small electronic devices, like cell phones, benefited by using Flectron for electronic shielding. Moreover, the pilot line was more than adequate for producing these smaller fabrics!

What happened to APM? Monsanto sold it to Laird. Marty Rapp, with a team of very smart people, completely redefined and rescaled the business. Today, APM is Laird Technologies. Laird Technologies, based in Chesterfield, Missouri, has plants around the world, and it brings in well over a billion dollars in revenue each year. Samsung is one of many of their large customers, and it's likely that Flectron is in the phone you are using today. Marty Rapp is the CEO of Laird. Laird is growing fast.

What happened to Monsanto? It dissolved. All the units were sold off or acquired: chemicals, fibers, pharmaceuticals, agriculture. Later, the company that bought the agricultural group spun off another company and called it the new Monsanto.

The powerhouse company I had briefly known, with all of the campuses, buildings, great buffets, large staffs, and great resources—the envy of any chemical engineering graduate—disappeared.

WHAT WENT WRONG AT TOYOTA?

First, it is important to understand Toyota within the entire context of the auto industry. The figure that follows shows the obvious shift that occurred. Every picture tells a story. GM has fallen apart over the last 30 years. GM's goal was to become the largest automaker in the world, and they succeeded. But in so doing, they became plagued with dams. When the dams caused the business to break, the people and the communities that had grown dependent upon a dammed GM suffered. As for Ford and Chrysler, they just didn't grow their share and they were more successful than GM, because they didn't lose as many customers. Toyota and Honda grew market share. It used to be the goal of Toyota to be the most profitable automaker in the world. And they became that. As GM collapsed, Toyota made the shift from wanting to be the most profitable, to wanting to become the largest automaker in the world. Was that a good want?

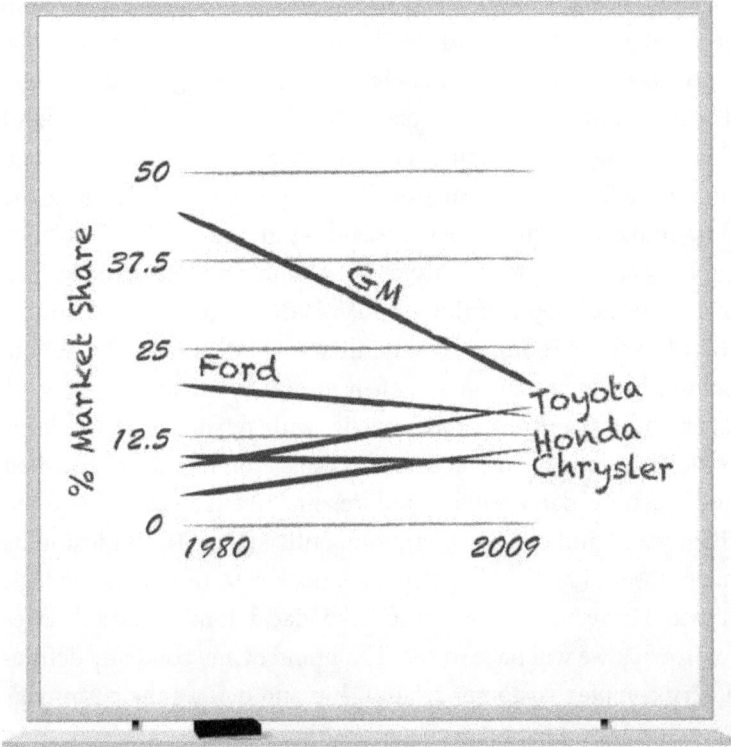

Figure 9: Global Automobile Market Share

So much of flow-thinking, as it relates to manufacturing tangible products, came from Toyota: the Toyota Production System or TPS and Lean Manufacturing, along with Kiazen. After World War II, they knew they couldn't afford to manufacture like GM. By doing more with less, they found what GM was doing was incredibly wasteful. GM had large inventories, large-scaled equipment, with a vast, complicated supplier network. GM didn't value how to use people's thinking, treated people as expendable machines, developed adversarial relationships between labor and management, and didn't understand the power of the work is social philosophy. Toyota did just the opposite and focused completely on the philosophy that work is social. GM had dams. Toyota had flow. Toyota has started to come undone in their quest to become the largest automaker in the world. Their ego dam has been obvious to the public recently. In many ways Toyota may have lost their magic.

As Toyota started to grow and become the number two automaker in the world (soon to become the number one automaker in the world) people began to wonder if the vaunted Toyota culture would be crushed by the sheer size and scale of their business operations. The upper echelons at Toyota had this same fear too: a real fear that they would lose it—lose the flow-thinking culture they created—and they did. What they experienced was the tragedy of the commons: they couldn't find and train the supply of flow-thinkers fast enough in order to run their business. Today, as I write this book, it appears the Toyota culture has been damaged in their efforts to become the biggest. There have been numerous recalls, with repairs in the billions of dollars, and the vaunted quality image of Toyota is tarnished and possibly damaged beyond repair. Toyota's quality defined their brand and created their competitive edge. Toyota losing its quality would be like the 1980 USA hockey team not having legs. It would have been a disaster in Lake Placid. It might be a disaster for Toyota; we will have to see. The brand of any company defines a very complex customer relationship and defines the customer's very complex buying decision. Hurt the brand and you do a surprising amount of damage to any business.

If Toyota did run out of flow-thinkers, then we should see dams developing in their culture. In the February 22, 2010, issue of *Time* magazine, entitled *Toyota Tangled,* we see Kiazen described thus: "In practice, it's the idea of empowering those people closest to a work process so that they can participate in designing and improving it." And they go on, "It is also about spreading what you've learned throughout the system. And then repeating it." In keeping with TPS, workers can shut down the line any time they see something they don't like; they would "call it out, figure out what it is . . . and convert ignorance to knowledge." This is all good stuff! The Toyota system is very simple and very complex. This is both good and bad—good in the sense that there are only a few things you need to do and focus on to make it work; bad because of its complex nature. If you miss some of the subtleties of the system, it all comes undone fast. Anything that looks and smells like a dam, does damage to the flow. Think of how the power of cavitation was neutralized by building a simple ramp in the Glen Canyon Dam spillways. Flows are powerful, but they can be easily diverted and dammed up, and flows have absolutely no tolerance for pollution.

One of Toyota's recalls was for brakes that were sticking. This problem spread across several models such as the Prius and the Lexus. Toyota had developed a very efficient system to use many of the same parts across many different models in order to turn a complicated materials flow into a simple one. This greatly reduced manufacturing costs. The problem is that if you don't manage the quality of the flow, you get a polluted flow, and this creates a disaster—fast. In Toyota's case, a multibillion dollar disaster.

The crisis originated when dam-thinking started to emerge and people started believing in fantasy and stopped paying attention to reality. As the article states, "When weak signals started coming in 2002, Toyota's top management wasn't listening. By then, the heroic stage of Japan Inc. was over; parts of its business culture had become sclerotic." If we take a trip to the dictionary we see that *sclerotic* means, "figuratively becoming rigid and unresponsive; losing the ability to adapt." And that, to me, looks like dam-thinking. What dams developed? As the article says, "Those lower in the organization find it difficult to deliver bad news to managers." When you have a communication problem like that you have a trust dam. Any other obvious dams? "Toyota is famous for having an arrogant culture. They're so used to dealing with successes that when they have a problem, they're not sure how to respond." Sounds like an ego dam. Toyota lost their ability to ask for help. When a CEO or business leader sees that in their own company, they better change it fast! And the Time article goes on with the nonsense: "Management cannot turn on a dime." Toyota has no choice. If they don't turn on a dime, a smaller, more nimble car company will come in and take over Toyota's place. Nobody can stop the flow of reality and the propensity of things to change. If you can't adapt and flow, your business fails.

As for the collapse of GM, GM should have been allowed to die long ago. If we continue to believe in "too big to fail" our US economy's ability to adapt will continue to erode and eventually erode our quality of life. We must let new companies emerge out of the failure of a large business entity. When a big tree falls in the jungle, the sun can can now shine on the small seedlings as they emerge and grow into healthy new trees.

STORY POINT 7:
The Size of Your Boat Determines Whether You Can Flow

Why do we insist on building big? The largest ocean liner in the world at this time is the Royal Caribbean *Oasis of the Seas*. This ship is 1,180 feet long, or 3.3 football fields, including all the end zones. It weighs 220,000 tons, which is just an unimaginable amount of weight. It carries 6,000 passengers and requires a crew of 2,000 people. It has a 100-megawatt power plant that burns through 12 tons of diesel fuel an hour. This is enough power for 105,000 homes. Just for the diesel fuel—assuming a $2.80 per U. S. gallon price for diesel oil—we are looking at almost $9,500 per hour. The fuel for a seven day cruise costs $1,140,000. If an average passenger pays $1,500 for a seven day cruise, it would take over 1,000 people just to pay for the fuel. The cost to build the ship was $1.4 billion. Depending on how the ship was financed, this would require large interest payments. Royal Caribbean goes by the stock symbol RCL. The total revenue for the company last year was $5.89 billion. The net income was $160 million. The total amount of debt according to the September 2009 balance sheet was $9.70 billion! The actual value of the company based on its stock price is $5.16 billion! The amount of interest expense at the end of fiscal 2008 was $327 million! This number will likely be higher at the close of 2009. On top of this, Royal Caribbean is building a sister ship to the *Oasis of the Seas* that will be launched sometime in 2011!

To manage a ship like the *Oasis of the Seas*, or for that matter, an entire company like Royal Caribbean, requires exceptional skill and sophistication. This is not a business for the faint of heart. One false move and everything comes crashing down hard. When you build big, there are usually surprises. For example, there were problems discovered only after Britannica, a precursor and sister to the Titanic, was built, which are documented in the book by

Brad Matsen, *Titanic's Last Secret*. When the Britannica was sent out under its own power the first time, engineers found that the ship's hull was vibrating in and out as if it were breathing, and it seemed like this vibrating threatened its chances of staying together. The engineers had to figure out a messy and costly solution. The hull was completely redesigned for the Titanic. The magnitude of the effect discovered on the Britannica was unexpected, just as the magnitude of the cavitation effect on the Glen Canyon Dam spillways was unexpected. Who knows what kind of engineering surprises occurred while building the *Oasis of the Seas* that couldn't have been predicted. When you build to a manageable scale, you can discover surprises early and learn. When you build big, it is risky and you have to have enormous confidence that you know enough to avoid disaster.

When I was at Monsanto, I remember sitting in some of the grand meetings we had in Building G (the business side where everyone wore expensive suits). In the first meeting I attended for APM, there appeared to be over 100 PhDs and many others like me filling the auditorium and everyone of them worked for our $3 million start up business, which the next week would have a massive lay off! I don't think the Manhattan Project had access to as many resources as when I first arrived at APM! The business manager for APM, Richard S. Olszewski, was giving a well-organized, slick, slide presentation. About halfway through he showed a slide of a relatively small electronic device, and then a huge chemical rail car. As I remember, he basically said Monsanto only understands the large scale of the rail car. They needed to understand the small scale potential of APM. Clearly, Richard understood the significance of scale and what it meant to business. And clearly, he was frustrated at the executive management at Monsanto for not appreciating his small-scale vision. Today Richard is the Executive Vice President of Speciality Products & Sales and Marketing at Louisiana-Pacific.

Because of the tremendous financial rewards, we are encouraged to be big. Businesses function best when they are scaled to perform at a human scale that all of us can see and understand. The businesses that do that have set themselves up for unlimited growth and can sustain themselves over many decades. When you make decisions to build to the correct scale, you pull very strongly against the ego dam and ensure a steady stream of productivity.

Figure 10: "Small Scale" Spider Diagram

What happened to Pan Am? If you watched the movie *The Aviator*, about the life of Howard Hughes, you would see that Juan Trippe, the CEO of Pan Am, was portrayed as a very egotistical, power-hungry man. Pan Am, founded in 1927, collapsed in 1991. It had built a huge skyscraper in New York City that was, for years, the largest commercial office building in the world. It was the first to order the biggest commercial plane in the world, the Boeing 747. Its initial order was for 25 of them! It had IBM build a huge computer that booked airline and hotel reservations and this computer took up the entire fourth floor of Pan Am headquarters. It built the largest airline terminal in the world at JFK airport. Why did Pan Am build big? Ego. Ego kills businesses.

CHAPTER 7

The Very Best Plan Never Survives the First Bullet

*Our lives improve only when we take chances—
and the first and most difficult risk we can take
is to be honest with ourselves.*

—Walter Anderson

"The very best plan never survives the first bullet," said Colonel Carl Schott, U.S. Army, and my former neighbor in Mesa, Arizona. Carl's saying hits right to the core. When I had a pigeon problem with the overhang over my front door, he told me to get a strong air gun and shoot the thing. I was worried about missing and getting hit from a ricochet. He simply said, "Practice. A soldier never misses his target." During my first spring living in Mesa, I experienced ash falling from a dark, midday sky. I wondered what it must have been like to have lived in Pompeii with Mount Vesuvius erupting, and there was Carl, standing outside in his army boots and casual attire, looking up at something that reminded him of battle.

The Lone Fire in the Four Peaks, Arizona, wilderness area was raging out of control, and firefighters were scrambling to find men and materials to combat it. Carl explained to me that facing this type of disaster was like a full prep combat assault, which he says was an "orchestration of precision." The artillery would be blasting the landing zone (LZ) and surrounding areas, and the gunships would be flying in. Just before the gunships reached the LZ, there would be a verbal code on one of the three FM radios and the artillery rounds would stop. The guns on the chopper would go hot and a cascade of ordinance would be delivered to the enemy. When the gunships landed, the doors would open and the soldiers would exit into an ever-expanding, ever-moving perimeter with everything—soldiers, gunships, ordinance, artillery, communication—happening in a flow.

In order to succeed in this type of operation, you needed the right equipment in the right place with experienced people serving drastically different functions, all communicating and making decisions in real time, and always focused on what they had to do to stay ahead. This was just like the firefighters battling the blaze.

The plan created a starting point. Everyone understood explicitly all of the objectives and the ultimate goal. This didn't change. What did change was the plan. Why? Because everyone was trained to deal with immediate reality—they had been trained to adapt and improvise. This orchestrated chaos required months of training, preparation, and repetition, after which every piece of information and every detail would be extracted during a postmortem analysis of the battle. Everyone strove to be better. As I came to learn via my many mountain bike experiences with Carl, he always drove himself to be better. Looking up at the fire,

Carl said that a full prep combat assault "was incredibly violent and incredibly beautiful."

The ability to plan is important. The plan is not important. Your ability to change plans quickly will allow you to improvise and adapt to the loss of a major customer, or a rapidly deteriorating economic environment, or a sudden change in technology, or a surprising competitive threat. Keep your mind fixed on the ultimate goal and your eyes focused on the immediate reality.

DEAL WITH IMMEDIATE REALITY

For many years, my fantasy goal was to ski the Baldy Chutes between Alta and Snowbird in Utah, an extreme and dangerous run that requires great skill. One of the steps to ski that level of terrain was to go well beyond my comfort zone and ski Alta's High Notch. Eventually, then, I would be skiing my fantasy run. Lee Praggastis, my friend and ski instructor, first took me up there on a windy day, and we side-slipped up on a thin rock ledge. Standing there, at well over 10,000 feet in elevation, not knowing what to do, I looked out on square miles of ski resort, mountains, and the distant horizon. Lee looked at me and asked, "Gray, what are you looking at?" And I said, "I am looking out and seeing everything and realizing how small I am." And I continued, "Lee, I don't know what to do. I don't know how I am going to make it down all the way to the bottom. I can't even conceive of a plan that will get me down. I have no idea where to start. I think you need to call a helicopter with a rope and fly me out of here." Lee, talking over a gust of wind that nearly knocked me over, said, "Gray, I can't do that. You are already committed. There is no way out of here but down." He continued, "Gray, quit looking at the horizon; look down at the bottom of this slope. That is where you want to get to, but that isn't important right now. There is only one thing that is important. Do you know what that is?" And I said, "Lee, I have no idea." Lee said, knowing that this was going to happen, "Have you not listened to anything I said all day?" I started trying to recall the day's theme.

When I ski with Lee he always has a theme, but I never thought it was that important. But right then, I knew I had to remember the theme because it was important to my survival. I thought fast. There is something about fear, the adrenalin going to your brain that allows what you learn while under its influence to be imprinted permanently on your memory. Lee knew this, and he wanted to be certain I had imprinted what I was about to say on my brain so that it would be there permanently for all time. Finally, I said, "Deal with immediate reality." Lee said, "Yes, Gray, the only thing that is important right now is that you deal with immediate reality, and what is that?" I said, "How to make the first turn." Lee said, "That's right. The only thing you should think about, the only concern you have right now, is how you are going to plan and make that first turn. Everything else doesn't matter."

I looked down to where I could see Lee step off the notch, jump down, execute one turn, and then slide a little bit to make room for me. As I looked at what I was about to do, and after I saw Lee do it, making one turn down this steep drop-off didn't look like such a big deal. I loosened up, held my breath, and jumped into my turn and stopped. I looked at Lee and he smiled and asked how I felt. I felt relieved. With that added sense of confidence, skiing down the rest of the slope wasn't that bad.

On my 50th birthday I skied the Baldy Chute. Lee gave me a little speech at the top. He said, "Ski the way you normally do. Don't try anything silly or unusual. People get hurt down this run when they think they have to do something different, overreact, or just do something stupid. Trust yourself. Ski exactly like you did on the runs this morning. There will be no problem. You will be fine." And Lee was right. I also knew him well enough to know he had concerns. He knew my success wouldn't be governed by my physical abilities or by my skill, but by my thinking. If I thought of myself flowing normally down the run I would be fine. If I thought of myself stopping and starting and being overly controlling and forcing everything—using dam-thinking strategies—the best case scenario would be a helicopter coming to pick me up so that doctors could attempt to put me back together again.

After Lee saw me ski the very top section he wasn't concerned anymore. He could tell instantly by my result, by the way I controlled my body, that I was thinking about this run correctly. If he had seen something different, he was prepared to shut things down as best he could. Instead, he turned away from me and quickly launched himself, zooming down to the bottom. He had complete confidence I would make it down safely. At that point, I was wide-eyed, not believing I was doing something that I had dreamed about for over 20 years.

As a beginner skier, cold and scared on a gray, snowy day on a narrow cat track in a bowl called Ballroom, I looked up at the bottom of the chute and watched someone ski down at me. At that time, I truly believed that skiing such a thing would be impossible for me to ever do. And that is why I set out to do it. I never gave up. And finally, after all that training, I did it. My plan was simple: find an expert, learn from him, and then go out and do it. You can accomplish a lot with your company with a big goal and a simple plan.

SUCCESS USING A SIMPLE PLAN

An ideal client for me is Mark Thomas, CEO at HEI. When we first met a few years ago, he told me how he had sent people down to his Tempe manufacturing facility, only to be told nothing could be done to improve the efficiency of the operation. He was told, "This is just how things are in this business." Because Mark was an outsider to the industry, he was horrified at these answers and absolutely refused to accept the industry *standard*. Mark wanted my honest assessment. The Tempe operation produced highly specialized, printed circuit boards that could be folded over (like an intricate model ship slipping into a bottle) and placed in very small devices, such as extremely sophisticated hearing aids. Within a couple of hours I had sketched the very complicated and messy movements of the material moving through the extremely disorganized plant floor. I then spent another couple of hours sketching out an organized plant floor, with a potential reduction in steps, estimated improvement in lead time, and estimated reduction in work-in-process inventory. Mark was sold. Nobody had made such a compelling case for how this plant could improve from such a messy operational environment.

After replacing the plant manager, overturning about 70 percent of the people, implementing flow initiatives (such as work cells, design of experiments (DOEs), and SCRUM), and having everything implemented with teams of workers, engineers, and supervisors, the facility became profitable. There was a reduction of work-in-process (the amount of materials on the floor required to build product) by 75 percent. The amount the plant could produce with a reduction of employees using essentially the same equipment doubled. The quality level went from 40 percent yield to above 70 percent yield on a steeply rising curve. Is the shop perfect? Not even close; but it is much better than it was. Improvements continue at an increasingly rapid pace. Teams that are accountable for results drive improvements at this plant.

Whereas the previous plant manager at the Tempe facility was pushing for a much larger facility, the management team at HEI today sees the Tempe facility as a scale model of how they want to duplicate other plants. The previous plant manager was absolutely involved in the tragedy of the commons, stripping the company of resources, and making customers increasingly upset and disappointed. When the plant converted to flow it shined.

WHEN IN DOUBT, SCRAP THE PLAN AND DEAL WITH IMMEDIATE REALITY

During the mid-1990's, as printed circuit board shops consolidated, they started to become very large businesses. AlliedSignal Laminate systems business was growing, but its customer base was shrinking with all of the consolidation. This consolidation made the business environment extremely risky. The loss of just one customer could be devastating. Combined with the increased commoditization of the industry across a vast range of technology, mainly driven by China's increased manufacturing capacity and abilities, the incentive to change suppliers was great. And so it happened. AlliedSignal Laminate Systems lost its biggest customer overnight! We were looking at disaster approaching at light speed.

Steve Hochhauser, the new president of AlliedSignal Laminate systems, and Bill Brandell, the new sales and marketing vice president, hatched a new plan without even blinking. Within 24 hours they calmly announced that they would attempt to become the primary supplier of Via Systems in Richmond, Virginia. Via Systems was the *Oasis of the Seas* of printed circuit board shops. The facility was huge and you could easily walk miles inside the building. Via Systems was locked up by one of Laminate Systems' prime competitors. Everyone wondered how it would be possible to displace this competitor. Steve and Bill knew that the market had become unstable. A supplier that could come in with a solution that would make their customers more profitable could steal away anybody's business. So that is what they immediately decided to do: to take 100 percent of Via Systems, laminate business. Steve and Bill had their eyes absolutely focused on dealing with immediate reality. Accordingly, Bill flew to Virginia within a day or so to find out whether he could close a deal. And he did.

Prior to losing the customer, the engineers at Laminate Systems had communicated to Steve's executive team that there was a way to make laminate materials very cheaply. It would require that the orientation of the panels would change 180 degrees. This would change the orientation of the woven glass along the width and length of the laminate. Woven glass has two directions: a machine direction where the glass fibers travel many hundreds of feet as they are spun out of bobbins, and a fill direction where they are threaded perpendicularly over and under the machine direction fibers. When the materials are laminated into a printed circuit board sandwich, the machine direction moves differently than the fill direction. In order for Via Systems to enjoy the low costs, all of the photo tools used to image the conductors on the laminate slices would have to be rescaled to accommodate the anticipated change in movement. Via Systems had many hundreds of different jobs with thousands of separate photo tools. I was given the assignment to put together a team to make the conversion happen within weeks or, at most, months. Via Systems engineers and lower-level managers had already reported back that it would take years. The deal would only happen if the conversion of the conductor artwork could be done quickly. I felt like I was standing on top of the high notch, wondering what to do, when I remembered: deal with immediate reality.

Via Systems had a model that predicted material movement based on theoretical equations derived from *assumptions* made about the physical properties of the system. It was an attempt at the perfect analytical solution. They were the same type of equations and assumptions I had learned about in Amundson Hall back at the University of Minnesota; the same type of equations and assumptions that were used to design the Glen Canyon Dam spillways; and the same type of equations and assumptions that UOP had tried to come up with in its attempts to build a perfect model for printed circuit board registration. Via Systems, which had close ties with Bell Laboratories, chose this same perfect analytical approach. Looking at the Via Systems model, I was reminded of my unit operations laboratory days in Amundsen Hall where we would get results that significantly deviated from the theoretical model. What I was looking at with the Via Systems model, to my horror, was that each product that was built had factors—called fudge factors—that adjusted the model to fit every single specific job in the factory! In essence, you took the result from the model, measured how the product deviated from the model, and then put a correction factor for that specific build in a table! Via Systems had pages of tables. The model was perfect mathematically, but in reality it predicted nothing.

Instead of relying on their model, I was going to have to start my work with the models that I had built up at Sanmina, using observations and data from small, compact, carefully planned DOEs. The type of model I used was based on multiple linear regressions. The only thing you need to know about regression models is that you just need data. You don't need to understand the physics, the chemistry, the crystal structures, the heat transfer, the fluid dynamics of melting epoxy liquids, the phase changes, the stored stress values and tensors, or any of the other physical effects that are all dependent on each other. All these effects are remarkably complex and need to be understood perfectly in order to derive the perfect analytical solution, but not necessary with an empirical model.

After looking at all of this, I still didn't have a plan—and I was constantly asked what my plan was by many people. I simply said, "I would like to hear your concerns and what you think needs to be done." And I would hear all sorts of excuses as to why changing to our material could never be done, because changing all of the imaging tools and collecting all the movement data would be too big, too expensive, and would take too long. I would let them talk and talk and explain—all the while saying very little. And then they would start in on it again. When they were spent I would ask, "But how would you proceed? What would be your first step?" I would ask, "What would be your first step?" over and over again. I was trying to get them to take their eyes off the horizon and just focus on dealing with immediate reality. I would have the team that consisted of Via Systems members and Laminate System members draft up a simple two-week objective to get the most obvious stuff done on time. We worked this way for a short time until the impossible started to look possible.

There wasn't anything remarkable or complicated about the plan. It was so simple. We ranked all of their production based on current volume. We looked at the material construction for these boards. We then designed a simple test vehicle to validate the movement for the construction using my regression model. As we did this multiple times, we began to gain confidence that we had devised a simple flow process that could rescale the majority of jobs in a couple of months—if that long. The team started to enjoy success. Via Systems was happy. And Laminate Systems was saved.

STORY POINT 8:
Use SCRUM and Immediate Reality to Tear Down
Organizational Silos

As Ken Schwaber, who developed the method along with Jeff Sutherland, says in his Google technical talk, which you can find on the web, "SCRUM is not an acronym, it refers to the game of rugby." In rugby a scrum deals with the uncertainty of who is going to get the ball. The ball is dropped into the center, players huddled together to move the ball, and what emerges is unpredictable, but what is certain, the ball does not sit still, the ball is moved!

In SCRUM think of the project as the ball. A cross functional team, which includes the customer or product owner, huddle together to create a prioritized list, which is a backlog of features for the product the customer wants. Based on the priority, the team divides the entire project into something called sprints: a tight 30 day, 15 day, 10 day, or even 5 day time box where they have to produce a working increment of product. You guessed it, you not only have to deal with the backlog and the priority given to each feature, but you also have to deal with figuring out how your going to manifest a fully functioning product with limited features at the end of each sprint! The sprints continue until the product owner is satisfied. Between each sprint, there is a planning session where changes such as adding new features or subtracting proposed features or any other changes can be added or subtracted for the next sprint backlog. At the end of each sprint there is a post-mortem to discuss what went well and what needs to be improved.

A key feature of SCRUM is the team meets daily for a short update to answer three questions: 1) what did you do? 2) what are you going to do next? 3) what are the roadblocks preventing you to get your work done? The amount of work a person needs to do is expressed in something called story points. A story point is a unitless metric that includes, among other things, the difficulty of doing the work, the level of coordination for the work, and the amount of time to get the work done. I like story points so much that I have used the name for the complex solution sections found at the end of each chapter. You might try to come up with a ranking based on difficulty (expressed using several parameters you choose) for each of the complex solutions discussed in this book in order to get a feel for story points. The burning down of the story points shows the percentage of completion for a task. This burn down is recorded in something called a burndown chart. You can tell if the team is on pace or behind after the very first meeting. SCRUM is very intense. SCRUM absolutely forces all issues to the surface. SCRUM forces everyone involved with it to constantly deal with immediate reality.

In one of my more recent SCRUM events, we had all of the engineering cubes torn down for my client. These were engineers that did their work strictly independently; worshiping the silo rituals of the My Precious dam. The intent of my destruction was to bring the engineers together and to get them to collaborate with each other as well as collaborate with the customer who they preferred to have as far away from them as possible. For example, when the customer engineers came to work with my client's engineers on their first sprint, the customer engineers were relegated to a side conference room. What I did was move the customers inside of the newly remodeled engineering workspace, at the large center table where they had access to several large whiteboards prominently displayed for everyone to see. All of the engineer work spaces formed a U cell around the table. Engineers started working with the customers at the large center table, and people started moving—going from the table, to an engineer's computer, to another engineer's computer, to the floor, and back. The timeline of what needed to be done that day was put on the center whiteboard. People were working on a roadblock and brainstorming on a recent problem that came up. Movement directed at dealing with immediate reality was happening.

All the pieces of the puzzle necessary to create this close colaboration that you need with SCRUM were put in place; the desire for a flow-thinking culture, the defined SCRUM project, the collaborative workspace, a customer with immediate needs and at their supplier site, and a spirit of working together outside of functional silos with an attitude of getting it done and dealing with immediate reality. The My Precious dam falls first with SCRUM.

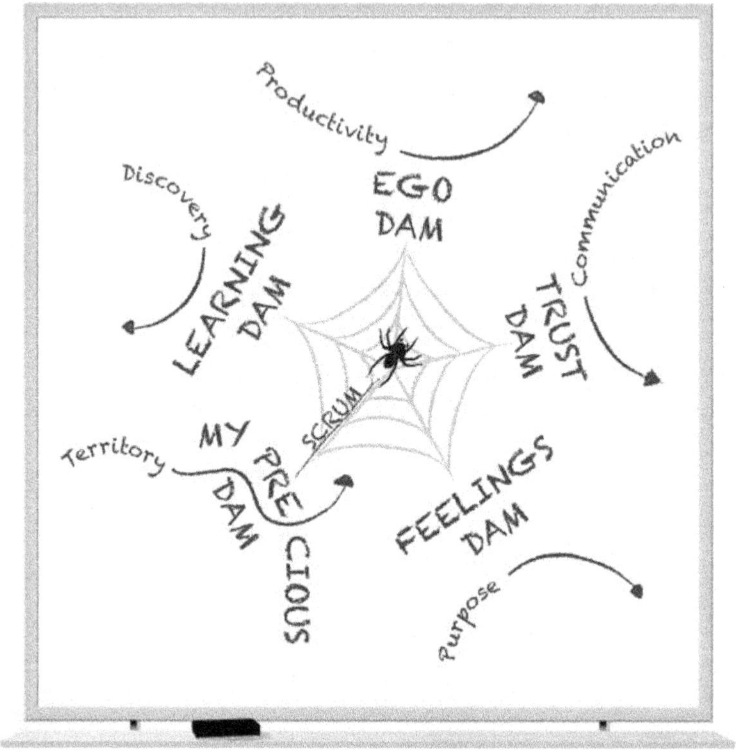

Figure 11: "SCRUM" Spider Diagram

A correct implementation of SCRUM will dissolve silos. The formulators of SCRUM, Schwaber and Sutherland, stress having a true SCRUM: people doing work on a single SCRUM project and nothing else. I find that is a very difficult thing for many companies to do for a variety of reasons. What I like to focus on instead, as a correct implementation and to maximize SCRUM as a truly complex solution to the My Precious dam, is to create the context and environment for the SCRUM team. I do that by setting up a SCRUM work area. The SCRUM team is assigned work time in that area. When they are in this area they can't be interrupted with anything outside the SCRUM project. In this way, the team not only has to learn to work together, they have to learn to plan together and live together. The individual members can also do other tasks outside of the team at specific times of the day. Scrum tears down silos and expands the individual and team territories.

CHAPTER 8

The Importance of Listening and Observing

---

*Don't underestimate the value of Doing
Nothing, or just going along, listening to all the
things you can't hear, and not bothering.*

—**Pooh's Little Instruction Book, Inspired by A. A. Milne**

After Beehive, I moved to Long Island, New York. Living in New York and working for Photocircuits, I learned to be loud, direct, and pushy. The way people interacted in New York was at first very strange for a Midwestern boy like me. But after awhile, it grew on me. I began enjoying the total freedom to just express what was on my mind. If someone irritated me, I would simply tell them a not-so-nice place to go. And they would retort back and, after a few volleys, there would be smiles, handshakes, and pats on the back. New York can be brutal, and New Yorkers enjoy being brutally honest. I came to believe that New Yorkers being brutal to each other, in a friendly sort of way, was a form of practice. Practice for the real work of getting people to move and getting something done. And after practice, you get a wink, a handshake, and sometimes a hug, to affirm it is okay. Being tough as soon as you walk in the door at 6:00 AM says, "We are tough. We can make it through anything." When you are accepted as one of them, a New Yorker, you no longer feel alone. You are part of a special club for life. I learned to love New York. I adapted. Perhaps too well.

After New York, I moved to the small city of LaCrosse, Wisconsin, to work for Norplex/Oak, later to become AlliedSignal Laminate systems. No two places could be more dissimilar. I needed an adjustment period, but it didn't happen. Making a move like this and immediately going to work was analogous to a deep-sea diver suddenly shooting to the top surface. With the sudden change from New York to Lacrosse, I was going through some serious decompression. My new boss, Bob Floyd, gave me an assignment just before he left town, to meet with the quality manger at the plant and have him explain everything they do.

The next day I traveled down to the plant, was showed around the quality laboratory, as well as the production areas and the in-process production test centers. I didn't like what I saw. I told the quality manager exactly what I thought, as if I were in New York. The quality manager heard me, because his whole head turned very red with veins popping out. I winked at him and thought to myself, "All in a day's work." I left the factory and returned to the building with my cozy cubicle office space.

When Bob returned from his trip, he called me into his office and in a calm voice he explained, "Gray, you have gotten the attention of everyone in the entire plant. This is not a good kind of attention. They want me to fire you." I was wide-eyed. He went on, "Gray, I blame myself for this. I should have coached you on handling people in a more genteel manner. After all, you came from New York. But that is all water under the bridge now." At this point, I really felt bad that I had let this man down. "Gray, the technical side of what you do is less than half of what you need. The more important side is how you treat and motivate people. I know you have it in you to master the people side. I am so confident in you Gray. So confident, in fact, that I know you can fix this yourself. Enough said. I am giving you a new assignment!" And he looked at me with a warm smile as he leaned over his desk. "When you leave this office, get on the phone and apologize to the quality manager down at the plant. After you do that, invite him to take a customer visit with you down to Rockwell Collins in Cedar Rapids, Iowa. I want you to ask for his help while you are there, and listen and observe everything that is going on. A simple assignment, don't you think?" Then there was a long pause as he looked at me intensely. Then he said, "Gray, when you take your trip, remember: *keep your mouth shut* and listen."

This talk turned out to be one of the most important lessons of my career—a talk I find myself coming back to in my dealings with other young and inexperienced engineers, managers, and supervisors. Nothing plugs up progress faster than an employee that thinks he or she knows the answer—a learning dam. When you have employees with both the ego dam and the learning dam operating, and they are totally defensive, refuse to listen, insist on wanting to be the expert, and pretend to have all of the answers, you have to take accountability and fire them. Sometimes this bad behavior may come from a consultant, senior engineer, or a bright and talented (but also arrogant) neophyte manager. Often, companies confuse arrogance, and the associated bad behavior, with confidence and competency. In time, the bad behavior will put your company in the disaster quadrant.

What saved me that day in Bob's office was I knew instinctively the issue was serious—I had done something terribly wrong—and I really wanted the opportunity to redeem myself. Arguing with Bob would have ended with my dismissal. I knew subconsciously if I listened, Bob would tell me how to redeem myself. He could see in my body language I was serious about what he was saying. He could see it in my eyes. He could see it by the fact that I was not saying a word. The behavior of staying quiet with the intent of learning how I could be better told him more than anything I had potential. Bob had every confidence I could solve the problem because of my silent listening behavior. I went to my phone, called the quality manager, and apologized with no pretext for defensiveness. I took full accountability for my behavior. I invited the quality manager to take a customer trip and he accepted. Clearly, Bob had done some negotiating and some groundwork behind the scenes. The behavior of burying your ego, taking full accountability, listening with the intent to learn, and then committing to an agreed-upon action and executing the action, is the exact type of behavior that will get anyone from any company very quickly on the right path with any dissatisfied customers.

Bob assigned John Dyer to be my mentor. John was from New Hampshire, so he understood my need to decompress from my New York experience. In fact, one of John's accounts was Photocircuits. So John understood the entire environment I had been subjected to. It was easy to follow John. He was older and had been in the business forever. He didn't have a technical degree. In fact, I don't think he even had a college degree. But he loved his work. Like water off a duck's back, he could deal with the toughest problems with ease. For John, it was all about common sense combined with a masterful ability to handle people. He was the best in the business.

John would take me into one of his accounts in which they were having serious difficulties and were really upset. We would go into a conference room and he would always have me sit to the right of him and make sure I sat close. He would ask the customer a question such as, "How are things?" or "How is business?" or "Tell me about your problem." And the customer would start in, red-faced and angry, about the problems. After a few minutes, I would catch something and would want to blurt out, "Wait that isn't right, you want to do this, and this should be done, not that, etc." And as soon as I wanted to speak, John would sense a change in movement from me and perhaps detect out of the corner of his eye the opening of my mouth, and, without missing a beat, and not looking at me, would gently but firmly wrap his hand around my forearm and squeeze. I would then immediately stop and relax and settle back in the chair. But I would look at John and say to myself, "John, why are you letting this go on? This customer is really screwed up with what he is trying to do. Tell him, please." But John just let him go and go and go.

After many visits like this, I began to observe something. Somewhere around the 40-minute mark the customer would start to tire and the intensity level would start to drop. The customer's face would start to turn white again. Sometimes customers began to realize, just by verbalizing everything that they were doing something wrong and the problem wasn't completely Norplex's fault! After the customer had nothing more to say, John would allow a long moment of silence. Then he would ask some questions such as, "When was the last time you had your lamination tooling plates reconditioned?" And the customer might say, "About two years ago." Then John might say, "Would you mind if I took a look at them to see if they are flat or bowed?" The customer would respond, "No problem." John would continue, "What press cycle are you running?" The customer might respond, "Let me call in my lamination engineer." Likely, the lamination engineer would say it was a very aggressive, fast-flowing, abrupt lamination press cycle that is used on their easy product. John might say, "For this more difficult product, would you mind if I suggest a different, less aggressive press cycle. Also, I would like to recommend using a different bonding sheet that has more resin in it, but will not flow as much, so that you get a better result. I have sent a package to your factory with some material I would like to test. Would you mind if we ran some tests after lunch with your engineer?"

The 40 minutes John had spent listening to the customer, uninterrupted, without the slightest hint of judgment, earned him the right to speak. John chose to use his right to be heard by focusing strictly on how to fix the problem. He didn't allow anything the customer said to hurt his feelings or distract him. He acknowledged that he heard the customer with silence, opting not to waste precious energy and time in an adversarial debate. Often, less is more! The only thing that mattered was the customer was ready to listen—and later, ready to observe the results that John and I had conducted. Sometimes, within a day, a problem that was aggravating the customer would be completely resolved. Most problems were resolved within two days. I began to realize, just as Bob had told me, that technical problems by themselves were easy. What makes technical problems difficult is dealing with people who will block you every step of the way if you don't allow them to be heard. If you know how to masterfully steer around these roadblocks or dams (by using simple tools such as listening and observing) you can make progress very quickly. This was my first hint that work is social.

THE POWER OF OBSERVATION

Frank Delk (from my Monsanto days) and I decided to embark on a similar experiment described by Barry Oshry in *Seeing Systems*. As you might recall from the *You Can't See Flow-Thinking with a Dam-Thinking Mind* section of Chapter 3, Oshry randomly assigns people top, middle, and bottom positions, puts them in the environment of a fictitious company, and then records the resultant happenings and behaviors. Conducting these events allowed Oshry to deconstruct the problems with traditional business systems, which I call a dam-thinking business culture.

Based on Oshry's work, Frank and I had a simple plan. We would create a traditional production system or dam-thinking system, run it, and film what people said and did. Then we would entirely change the production system to a flow system, run it, and film what people said and did. During the event, we encouraged the participants to observe and learn with us. We didn't know what to expect. What happened was completely consistent with the theory of broken windows mentioned earlier in this book. Our environment, the context, the rules, and the organization of our workspaces strongly affect our behavior! This has huge implications on what you need to do to fix your business!

We borrowed from a training method used to convince people of the superiority of the Toyota Production System (or, Lean). To review, the intent of the TPS is to eliminate all unnecessary activities that don't contribute value to the manufacture of a product. One important idea in this system is to bring all the equipment tightly together in a U-shaped cell in the right way, which would result in large increases in efficiencies, throughput, and quality. In order to force people to buy into the idea of using work cells, and to demonstrate the fallacies of their current thinking, many consultants would force people to build toys, simple clocks, or some other non-real world widget, in both a traditional factory and in a flow factory using work cells. Many Lean consulting companies have thought that just doing this simple toy exercise would be enough for workers to see the value of a work cell. But it almost always fails to change people's minds or cause them to accept a more flow-thinking structure. If it did, there would be so many other well-run companies such as Pixar, Apple, and Southwest Airlines.

Frank and I knew from experience that a simulated result wasn't enough to convince people. There were two reasons why we thought this. First, it is too difficult to make the translation from a simple toy to an actual complex production assembly. Second, people will only see what their minds let them see. They won't see the better flow result if their minds are in a dam-thinking mode. For example, people may just feel manipulated by a simple toy example, wherein they can't exert any of their own decision-making authority. In order to have any hope of changing people's minds, people must be given a choice of which system is better. They must be given a choice of how to use their own dam-thinking and watch it fail on their own terms. Keeping the exercise predictable, by definition, was a manipulation. Keeping the demonstration predictable meant it was dam-thinking. You can't understand flow-thinking by applying dam-thinking principles! The result is no dam progress. There is no need to observe anything or learn anything because the outcome was known before the event even started! The dams involved in these types of demonstrations are the ego dam of the consultant, the trust dam among the students, and the learning dam of everyone.

Frank and I undertook the use of toys in a different way. We wanted to uncover people's change in thinking and videotape what they did, what they said, and how they behaved. We wanted a very social context for our event. We wanted them to not only build the toys and be observed, but also to participate actively in our learning and discoveries. Knowing this up front generated much excitement and enthusiasm by all of the participants. Everyone knew that each person had his or her role, but we were all equals working together. We really didn't know what would happen or what we might learn. Creating a situation that had an unpredictable outcome—in which something new would likely emerge—meant we had met a very important requirement for flow-thinking.

This event had everyone observing: themselves, each other, the system, and the environment. Often, people get themselves in trouble by filtering what they are observing—sometimes to the point that they deny reality and choose fantasy. Few job descriptions stress a need for unbiased observational skills. Such skills just aren't valued. We prefer action and activity. The passive, tedious, and boring discipline of observing seems to be just a waste of time to us. I have sat in the corner of a factory and observed for hours stretching across many days. I have babysat processes overnight, not doing anything but watching. Yet, the time I spent was invaluable. My grandfather understood the power of observation when he had the schoolteachers watching his factories. Their observations were much more valuable than the numbers they were collecting. When the registration team ran all of those experiments at Sanmina, the team walked every experimental panel through every process step, taking very careful notes. When Sanmina had its October Surprise disaster, the team was ready to find and then implement the permanent fix in less than 24 hours. Few things are as powerful as listening and observing.

The goal for the event that Frank and I had organized was for a team of eight people to assemble as many Lego block dinosaurs as they could in a 40-minute time period. This was a toy that could be assembled by a six-year-old in four minutes. How well would a group of intelligent adults assemble this toy organized in a traditional factory? Would changing to a work cell and changing how the work was organized have any positive effect? Would it change people's behavior?

We started with a traditional factory full of dams. The first thing that we did was deliver all of the parts at once. The assigned materials manager was responsible for organizing all of the parts into large bins. She quickly became frustrated. She didn't want to give anyone any parts until she was done organizing. She didn't see that her need to protect her *my precious* territory was causing a problem. She saw what she was doing as her right—a right that others were not respecting. Because each person doing assemblies quickly distrusted the materials manager's ability to do her job, each assembler ordered too much of the material that was needed. Quickly, with the chaos in the materials room, it became every person for themselves. The materials manager quickly began to complain, became unhappy, and didn't think well of anyone. The assemblers were, in a very short period of time, behaving badly. Everyone was treating each other badly. Nobody was happy—the customer, the quality manager, and the supplier were indifferent and apathetic. All of this bad behavior started to emerge in a span of less than eight minutes!

After fighting for their parts like rabid dogs, the assemblers started building away. There was a high degree of technical dependency required between the assemblers, because the work required manufacturing sub-assemblies and then combining these sub-assemblies in the final step. But, the dog-eat-dog competitive environment discouraged the required collaboration for successful assembly. As a result, when the time came to put all of the assemblies together, there was confusion, mistakes, inventory shrink (lost parts), and scrapped parts. After 20 minutes, with the quality manager complaining to everyone about her job, nothing was getting done. After 35 minutes, one dinosaur was completed. It was in such a visually shabby condition that it was returned by the customer. Not a single adequate dinosaur toy, a toy that a 6 year old in a few minutes could put together, was assembled after 40 minutes, using eight very smart, accomplished, and capable people.

At the end of this first exercise, everyone thought that everyone else was completely incompetent. They all liked each other, but after the traditional factory floor exercise was over, they didn't think much of each other at all. When they were walked through the problems that occurred in each area, but where the systemic issues weren't revealed, they came up with ideas for adding more workers, beefing up quality and inspection, having more people sorting the materials, and so on—all standard dam-thinking tactics. They wanted to create a classic tragedy of the commons, which was discussed in chapter 2.

Frank and I wanted to capture the change in people's thinking before and after the event. Before the event, each person was asked to rank what they thought was most important for the success of a business. For example, many people thought a person's skill, the desire to do good work, and a quality mindset were most important. What every person thought wasn't important was the organization of the factory, making work instructions simple and visual with minimal words, the ability for people to socialize and work together, being able to see each other's work, being able to do many different functions, the ability to observe and learn, and accountability—all these things were considered unimportant!

For the next exercise, the quality manager was removed. Half of the assemblers were removed, leaving only two assemblers. The work was organized around a U cell instead of separate individual work stations. The two assemblers started at the last assembly step, put together a dinosaur, and then moved backward through the process. You had the flow of the work running forward while the assemblers were moving backward. This is known as a counter current workflow and may be difficult to visualize, but it does work. The two assemblers working as a team completed 25 high-quality dinosaurs in 40 minutes. The way everyone interacted and behaved, even those on the sidelines, was remarkable at its level of collaboration. This change happened in less than an hour!

When asked to rank again what was important, people said the organization of the factory floor, the design of the work instructions, and the ability to work together as a team that was communicating all of the time and trusted each other were most important! This was a huge change in mindset that occurred in hours not years! What was surprising was most people didn't think their thinking had changed from before the event to after the event! When our thinking changes it is very difficult for us to remember how we used to think. It is as if we had thought in the new way from the beginning.

Changing our thinking is a tricky business. All of us have blind spots. We have to observe and be observed. We have to examine how we think now and compare it to how we thought before. We have to have an undisputable record and data. And we need time to digest it all. In time we begin to think comfortably in the new way, as if it were the way we thought all along. This is the power Chris Argyris talks about with his writings, which describe second order learning. Second order learning is your path to go from dam-thinking to flow-thinking.

STORY POINT 9:
Observe . . . No Operator at Station: Code 19!

When I walk into a factory or a business that has problems, I am often amazed at how few people actually go out and observe the process. A typical excuse is, "We don't have time, we need action now!" Action in and of itself is not a good thing. Mindless actions will lead to disaster. If you want to make an improvement right now, stop issuing actions. Go out to the workspaces. Observe and listen and begin to discover and understand.

At AlliedSignal we were involved in a Kiazen event to help one of our large customers. The goal was to straighten out incoming material, material preparation, material surface cleaning, and imaging. The customer felt that more imaging equipment, more cleaning equipment, and more operators were needed. They were, of course, wrong. They had too much of everything already. The manager of this area of the factory knew he had production problems, but didn't know where to start or how to proceed. So we decided to put together a simple audit sheet. The audit would be done twice a shift across three shifts. There was significant resistance to the audit. They didn't see the point since they already knew what was going on. Or so they thought.

Every time an audit was done, there were several stations with no operators! This was Code 19 on the audit form! The manager was furious. At first, the manager wouldn't accept the data. He could not believe that operators would deliberately disobey his direct order to stay at their stations. After several supervised visits to the plant floor with me, he began to see that the Code 19 data was accurate. But the reason didn't appear to be insubordination; it was something else altogether.

During the subsequent Kiazen, the team listed each step an operator actually performed in order to produce product. This will always be significantly different than a written operator procedure. After the actual steps had been identified, each step was marked on a scale drawing of the factory floor plan. The location of these steps was connected into something that looked like strands of spaghetti—in fact, the diagram is called a spaghetti diagram. When we did this for the Kiazen, we learned that the operators had to perform some 180 tasks and walk over a mile to produce a small number of panels! The actual value-added tasks, or the tasks used to make product, were less than 20 steps!

Deconstructing the reasons for all of the steps was analogous to an archeological dig. With each serious problem that occurred in the production area over many years, engineers and managers put checks and added procedures to make sure the problem or event would never happen again. They were trying to apply localized improvement, like the spider at the edge of its web, which produced more work for the operator and delivered little (if any) benefit. The spaghetti diagram revealed the insanity of it all. Artwork checks, machine checks, paperwork everywhere, getting supplies, checking supplies, filling out forms, waiting for other people—all of it put in place without any thought.

The spaghetti diagram spoke to what needed to be done. The whole area was reorganized, support roles for the operators were defined and implemented, and the operators became extremely productive and remained at their stations. This company wasn't yet ready to have operators move as a team within a work cell.

You might think the first dam to fall when you implement a policy of listening and observing would be the learning dam. The dam that usually falls first though, is the trust dam! I have sat in a corner, followed work around the floor, and after awhile, an operator who starts talking to me. It might take an hour for this to happen, or a day, but never longer than a week. Soon, other operators start talking to me, showing me things, explaining things, and I don't even have to ask a question. This builds trust fast. Soon, supervisors, the support people, and vendors will start talking too. People start to trust your ability to lead them through change when you have spent the time to listen to them and observe the way they work.

Figure 12: "Observation" Spider Diagram

You might think that observation would pull on the learning dam first. I have never seen it happen this way. When I spend a significant amount of time observing a process operation, not saying a word, not giving any sort of command, or passing on any type of judgment, people are attracted. If you watch in this way, it shows you care. People want to come up to you and ask what you might need, or what you are seeing, and they will be motivated to show you and help you understand. It is a program that is part of everyone's psychology. We just can't help it. We instinctively trust people who sincerely want to learn what we do, and we want to help them see how they might help us. Observation skills are underutilized in business today and, as a result, few businesses have a truly trusting workforce. As Earl Bakken said, my grandfather knew how to develop trust and motivation. My grandfather spent a lot of money and time observing Green Giant's operation. And it was worth every minute and every cent.

CHAPTER 9

The Art of Improvising

My future starts when I wake up every morning...
Every day I find something creative
to do with my life.

—**Miles Davis**

Jazz and improvising go hand in hand. The album *Kind of Blue*, by Miles Davis, remains the greatest jazz album, and it is considered by most music critics to be the best album ever made. The album was created in just two days. The first recording day was March 2, 1959, and the second recording day was April 22, 1959. There were no rehearsals because there wasn't anything to rehearse. Sure, Miles walked in with a few chords just before they recorded, but that was it! Amazingly, when they started to play, it was as if the music was simply extruded onto the master tape. The music seemed preformed. It was perfect. Trying to recreate the performance, or leaving a musician out, or changing the tempo of the music would have completely changed the result. The effort was truly complex. Not only does *Kind of Blue* represent the highest standards of improvisation, but it also defines the truly complex and emergent nature of creativity.

Key to the greatness of the session was the caliber of the people. At the session you had John Coltrane, Bill Evans, Wynton Kelly, Jimmy Cobb, Paul Chambers, and, of course, the leader, Miles Davis. In order to have great people you have to attract them. Miles attracted great talent. First, he had a reputation for creating great music. Second, he supported his musicians. For example, he set up John Coltrane to be his own leader with his own group creating his own music. Third, he was a great innovator. Fourth, the very best musicians were attracted to him because they too wanted to be part of something that would change the face of music forever. And the album *Kind of Blue* did that.

As a dam-thinker, we have a hard time seeing and understanding an improvised jazz performance. We can't understand how the musicians can be making spontaneous decisions while playing together, and still sound so coordinated, precise, and good. It just doesn't compute. Plus, the reason to improvise seems so unnecessary. Why not write the music out and rehearse it? Wouldn't that be better? Be more consistent? And have higher quality? Dam-thinkers control, but never improvise. In so doing, they never learn. Jazz musicians jam, because they know something new will emerge, even though they may have played the same song hundreds of times.

In a Fortune magazine article I read once, Win Wallin, the former CEO of Medtronic, was asked about the wisdom of a young manager getting an MBA. He said something like, "Skip the MBA. You would be better off learning jazz clarinet." This seemed flippant when I first read it, but he was really saying a lot in that statement. In fact, as I have come to learn, the ability to improvise isn't a nice thing to be able to do, it is an absolute requirement for managing a complex business using a flow-thinking paradigm.

The ability to improvise comes from mastery and discipline. Coltrane, for example, spent, at times, 16 hours each day practicing his horn and working on his music. After concerts, he would immediately walk off the stage, go to his room, and practice for hours. He would wake up, put on his robe, pick up his horn, and practice. He would drive with his saxophone at his side, holding the steering wheel with one hand, while working out complicated chords and fingerings on his horn on the other. The message? If you are going to be a good improviser, be prepared to do a ton of work in terms of developing skills and mastering them. If your people aren't reading, learning, going to seminars, working on their skills at work and at home, and working with each other on ways they can be better, you will not be able to have teams that can improvise. You won't be a flow-thinking company. Improvising isn't about being careless. It is about being extremely mindful and aware.

When Davis started to assemble the people that would create *Kind of Blue,* many years before the recording he had them practice in his Greystone home just off Central Park. He spent weeks listening to them play through his hallways and intercom system. He wouldn't play with them. He wanted them to learn how to become a group so that their collective musical voice would be strong and independent. Miles wanted a tension, almost a clash, in styles—a clash that would have to resolve itself every time they played together at a club or on a recording. Nothing Miles did had anything to do with consensus. In fact, there wasn't even a meeting to discuss what they should do. There was no plan. They just did it. And they listened. And they learned. Together and by themselves. Silently, and in their own way. Miles, by his initial lack of participation, became the prod, just like Herb Brooks. Everyone wondered when they would be good enough for Miles to join them. Herb was vocal in his demands. Miles was silent. But they both did the same thing: they completely removed the feelings dam. What Miles did was filled with tension. It was kinetic. And in the end, what emerged was something magical—*Kind of Blue.*

Kind of Blue is considered to be Davis's greatest album. Yet, it was an album Davis was disappointed in because it didn't emerge the way he thought. He forgot that each musician had unique ideas. He forgot just how unpredictable things would become with such a powerful team of musicians. As much as he wanted the album to be different, he forgot that he long ago had given up control when he pushed improvisation to limits never before seen. Miles, as great a flow-thinker as he was, struggled with who should get credit for the work. The ego dam wasn't completely removed from Miles or the other musicians, and hence, they didn't enjoy the end product as much as they should have. We are all human. We all suffer at various times and to different degrees from the thinking dams that make up our DNA. Even when we know better.

QUALITY CIRCLES

Almost all business quality improvement initiatives, such as Total Quality Management, Six Sigma, and Lean, aren't based on flow in their implementation scheme, but on dam-thinking and control. First, there is a very well-described system with many detailed steps that must be followed to the letter. Second, the plan is all-important, cannot be changed, and must be followed. Third, all-important decisions are made by a leader who typically is the least skilled and least experienced in the group. Fourth, everyone is supposed to be patient and wait for the outcomes, which are supposed to happen in the distant future. Every business improvement initiative I had to endure with others never broached the subject of improvising. These initiatives were always dammed right from the start.

My first experience with a business improvement initiative was Quality Circles back in 1982 with Beehive in Salt Lake City, Utah. The Quality Circles concept was meant to be a way for workers to improve business results through implementing their own ideas. It was supposed to get workers more involved and make them more engaged. It was simple and to the point. Unfortunately, Quality Circles can't work in a dam-thinking culture. And Beehive, as we learned, was dammed.

Like many improvement initiatives in the 1980's, Quality Circles came out of Japan, and like so many things that come out of Japan, something gets lost in the translation. Beehive management had a preconceived idea of what the workers would come up with to improve productivity. This is natural. It's just like Miles and his preconceived ideas of what would emerge from the *Kind of Blue* recording session. In Beehive's case, these preconceived ideas proved fatal to the initiative.

After many weeks of working with their Quality Circles coach, the ideas that the workers came up with revolved around how to make their work environment better and more organized. When this was presented to upper management, they were disappointed. They wanted to see a business case, not a purchase requisition for new lockers! After the coach told the team that all of their ideas were rejected and nothing would be done, the workers were livid. They chased the poor coach all the way out to the parking lot and to his car. That was the last I saw of Quality Circles at Beehive.

The lesson to be learned was that management felt there was a difference between the work environment—a cleaner, more organized, and happier work environment—and working longer hours—slaving away and getting more done in less time. Management didn't understand that making a better work environment, where workers felt pride in ownership, would have been the first step to building real, sustainable productivity improvement. Management was use to the complicated linear approach. What they didn't realize was the right answer: the nonlinear complex approach that was emerging out of the Quality Circle meetings. For example, if management approved their plan, it would have immediately changed the way the workers perceived their factory environment, their role in the business, and their impact on the company. It would have produced a never-ending stream of changes that would emerge and dramatically make the company better. None of this happened at Beehive, because of managements' preconceived notions.

SIX SIGMA WORKS IF YOU TURN IT UPSIDE DOWN

Six Sigma was the quality initiative of the 1990's. Larry Bossidy pushed it at the time I worked at AlliedSignal. I was trained in it. Six Sigma is a great training program, but it isn't a very efficient business initiative that changes companies. It is expensive. You have to wait a long time to see results, which typically aren't sustainable. The nature of the hierarchy from green belts to black belts to master black belts, which is supposed to denote your command and application of the material, creates division and discord and tends to encourage My Precious dams, ego dams, and trust dams. In order to be effective, I had to break the rules of Six Sigma.

The way many consultants start a Six Sigma effort is with detailed process maps or value maps, and before you know it, things get complicated fast. The way I start a Six Sigma effort is by listening to people's stories. The stories describe a system of beliefs, and within those beliefs, assumptions, rules, and paradigms are revealed. Combining the stories with parallel thinking strategies starts to reveal the underlying issues; it also maps out the current thinking of the team. Chronic problems demand a change in thinking in order for them to be solved. Chris Argyris, a highly distinguished MIT professor, introduced the principle of double loop learning a long time ago. According to Argyris, we have a theory in our mind, or what he would call the theory-in-use, which often is called a paradigm by others. In single loop learning we simply correct an error, but keep our original theory intact. In double loop learning, we change the way we see and think about the world! Solving technical problems is always about solving people problems. As Bob Floyd told me time and time again, "Gray, solving the technical part of the problem is easy. Solving the people part is why you will be paid."

When I was summoned to a large customer of AlliedSignal Laminate Systems to solve a problem of electrical shorts caused by bad alignment of the drilled holes with the circuit image—bad printed circuit board registration—I listened to the stories and what people were telling me. With my upside down version of Six Sigma I started the stories by having them rank what they thought was important. Then I turned this list upside down and had them justify the least important items.

The first item that didn't score high in the ranking was artwork accuracy. From their stories, people *believed* the artwork was good. Yet, there were observed, significant errors to the artwork dimensions—bad artwork! These were viewed as aberrations or one-time events. Anytime I hear this in anything I do, I stop and pay attention. I just don't believe in aberrations. Almost always the person is rationalizing his or her *theory of use*. A view that, if not corrected, may contribute to a disaster. The need to protect the current view creates blind spots. We all have blind spots, which is why we all need to challenge each other's thinking. Two heads prove to be better than one.

The second item that didn't score high in the rankings was the punch accuracy. The thin, rigid fiberglass material that is used for the circuit sandwich slices has to be punched very accurately, and these punched holes are called tooling holes. For example, one hole may be punched on the right and one hole on the left. These holes align the circuits as they are layered and stacked, one on top of the other.

The punch had my attention because, in my audit, each plotted data set showed all of the panels were rotated! I asked the engineer what he thought. He said, "I see that all of the time. It doesn't fit with what I understand the punch to be doing. I think something is fundamentally wrong with the gauge." This gauge excuse looked to me, once again, as a rationalization for their *theory of use*.

When you conduct a meeting that challenges assumptions, you have to be persistent with questions—questions that have *what* in them. For example, "You can't control the supplier, so what can you control?" Or, "What about the artwork? If the artwork doesn't have accurate dimensions, what would happen? On top of that, what would you do to aim at your target?" The team decided after a little while that it was worth collecting a meaningful data set that would reveal the true variation in the artwork dimensions so that they could prove to me the artwork was good.

I also started asking, "What about the tooling punch? Do we have any data on this?" And I would get back, "But it isn't important because we know there isn't a problem there. We know what the problem is! It is Allied's material! Why are you wasting our time?" And I would say back, "But how do you explain the in-process data?" And they would respond, "But that isn't a good gauge." And I said, "What if the story the gauge is telling is right? What then?" And they all agreed that they needed to collect data to prove to me that the punch was good.

The artwork dimensions were not accurate. The punched tooling holes were misaligned, showing a serious rotation. There was complete and utter disbelief by many people. Only after allowing people to challenge, collect their own data, do their own analysis, did everyone come to understand the real issues and what needed to be done. Defining the problem correctly always reveals the true solution. But the discoveries made shook the confidence of many people. That is because they were still in a dam-thinking paradigm. Most of us aren't trained in double loop learning—in fact, just the opposite. We are taught not to expect outcomes that will cause our thinking to change. This is especially the case if we have been taught by dam-thinkers who just want you to learn what is already known, instead of how to learn and make new discoveries about the nature of complex things.

STORY POINT 10:
Your First Jazz Lesson!

Improvising is about skill, mastery, and process. The fuel of improvisation involves a very minimal set of ideas. It's strange to us non-jazz musicians, but jazz musicians live for rules and constraints. They learn to play inside (inside the rules) and outside (outside the rules) and you will hear them talk about playing inside and outside in their conversations. When a jazz musician plays a concert at a club with really good musicians, they leave the stage not only physically exhausted, but also mentally exhausted. I was schooled in improvisation by a number of different teachers. In my early thirties, I really wanted the mystery of improvising to be revealed, because I thought it was so magical. When I happened to walk into a music store near Westborough, Massachusetts, one day, I decided to take a few lessons. When I worked at Monsanto, I took a jazz ensemble class at Webster University and learned what goes on between musicians and how they communicate musically back and forth. Before that, the better part of my training consisted of many years of study with Tony D'Aveni in his basement in Worcester, Massachusetts.

Tony had a dream to learn and record great jazz trumpet music. He was also highly motivated to compose his own music. At the age of 18, he entered North Texas State University and was in their world-acclaimed big band. Later, he would study at the Berklee College of Music in Boston and play with artists like Art Farmer, Rob McConnel, Dick Johnson, and Bobby Shew among others. He listened to great trumpet players such as Chet Baker, Kenny Dorham, Miles Davis, Tom Harrell, Lee Morgan, and Clifford Brown. Tony would spend hours a day doing nothing but listening. He would transcribe solos note for note. He would have much of the music on reel-to-reel tape and sometimes would turn the tape slowly with his hand so he could hear exactly how a trumpet player, such as Clifford Brown, used his tongue to produce and release the note. He would study every nuance, every articulation, every breath. He would listen to the music with headphones while he fell asleep. When Tony first heard me play, he told me, "Gray, you have at least 10 years of listening to do."

Tony would take small sections of musical notes from a transcribed solo. Such notes are musical words and parts of musical sentences. Tony would memorize them. Not as notes, but as numbers or digits that represented their location on a scale. Then he would play them in every key and in every scale from major to minor, from augmented to diminished, starting from every degree, with every chord inversion. He would permute the order of the notes in every possible variation. His practice time went from two hours a day, to six hours a day, to twelve hours a day, and beyond. A musician like Tony can practice in his or her mind, and often does so. So even if they are working or doing another job, they are thinking about their music. After getting a few musical ideas down in every possible way, Tony would then practice these ideas over the chord changes of songs, or standard chord progressions called cycles, or different types of turnarounds (a turnaround is how, after leaving your starting chord, you can return safely to the orginal chord). Tony would work every possible combination and permutation.

To give you an idea, think of a simple II, V, I chord progression. You hear this progression all of the time across all types of music. Most people learned a C-major scale in school. The most basic of all digitized ideas (numbers instead of notes) are 1, 2, 3, 5 or, simply, 1235. You see this 1235 idea overlayed on the C major scale depicted below:

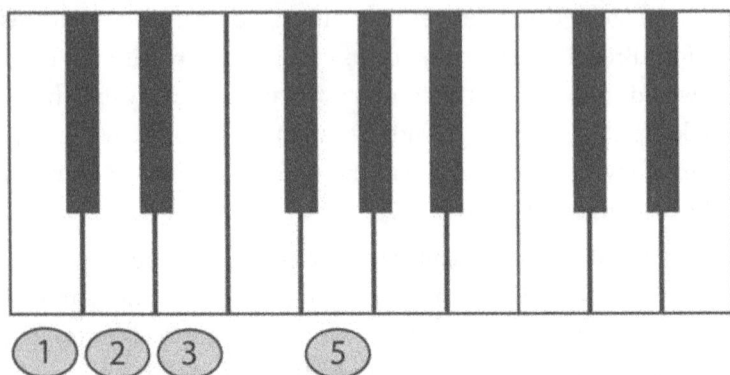

The II chord, simply starts on D but stays within all of the notes of the C major scale, which is all of the white keys. In the figure below I overlay the 1235 idea over the II chord. Changing where you start within a scale defines a mode to that scale. As a side note, Miles exploited this idea of using different modes of a scale instead of complicated chord changes, and he did that in *Kind of Blue.* This type of jazz is called modal jazz. Even though George Russell really created modal jazz, Miles is given much of the credit for its invention.

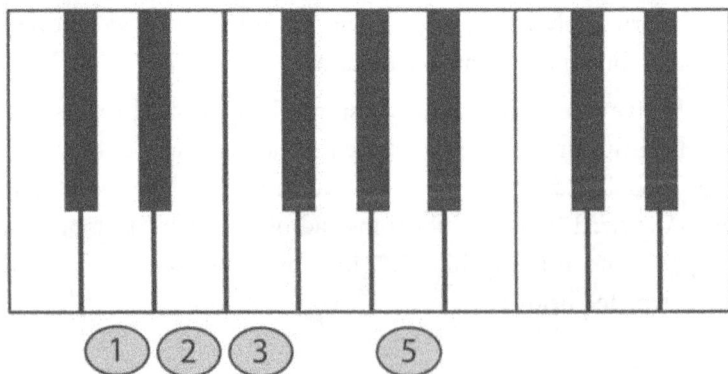

When you play the II chord, you have a completely different sound and a different feel than the I chord. In fact, the I chord is major and the II chord is minor! This demonstrates how a slight reorganization of where you start and where you end can produce a significantly different feel and result. That is why a flow thinker is very mindful of the materials he or she has and the order in which things are done; he or she is always searching for the best way to organize things. This is the type of thinking that is required from a musician, an artist, an architect, and anyone involved with design. As a CEO who wants to design a company that flows and grows, you have to start to see yourself as an artist.

The V chord is shown in the next figure with the 1235 idea. So, all you have to do is play the 1235 starting with the II chord, then the V chord, and ending with the I chord.

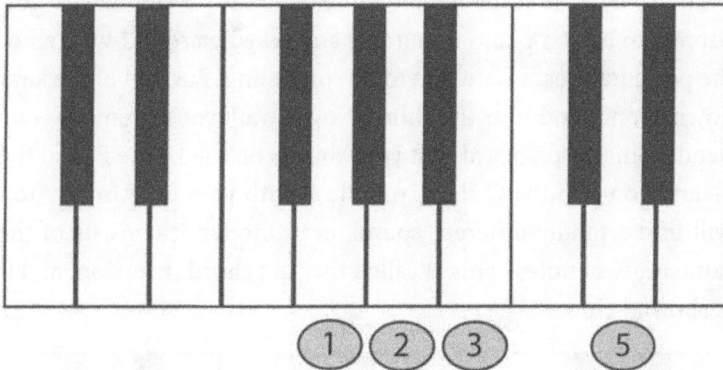

This may seem boring and simple to you right now, but this lesson has been well-traveled by many of the greats, such as Coltrane. They all started right here, and none of them ever forgot this lesson because this is the lesson from which all else builds. Believe it or not, just this information alone can generate countless hours of practice. Just like in an improvised solo, you don't need a lot of ideas to make your company unique and great. Often, less is more.

Just sticking to the 1235 idea, how many ways can you play this? For example, you could play in the order 2351, or in another order, 2315, and so on. You use something called a factorial to figure the number of possible combinations. In this case, the factorial is denoted thus: 4!. The number 4 is used because there are four notes. This factorial is then solved by multiplying the numbers in succession, or 4x3x2x1, which is 24. There are 24 unique ways you could play this simple idea, starting with C at the bottom of the scale! But are those all of the possibilities? If you happen to be at a piano doing this and playing around with all of the permutations, I want you to do something. Push all of the keys down at once and hear the chord. Now, I want you to remove your hand from the keyboard. Put your thumb on the D, the E, and the G, and go up to the C above middle C with your little finger. You will find a totally different sound, even though it consists of the same musical notes! This is called the first chord inversion, and it is shown below:

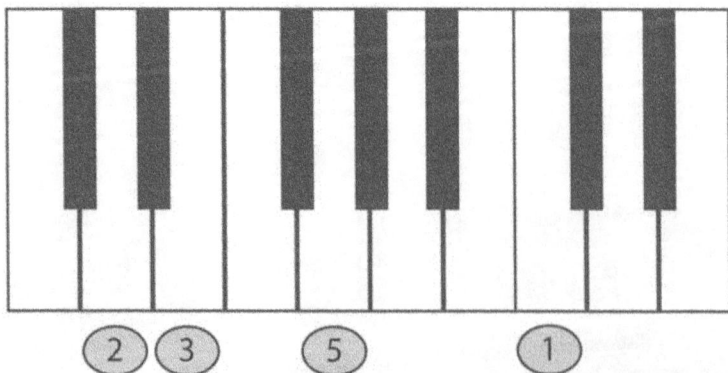

Guess what? There are now 24 new ways you can play the 1235 idea. Is that all? No, there are two more chord inversions. There are 24 x 4, or 96 different ways to play 1235, and hundreds of ways to play 1235 over the II, V, I chord progression. And this is just the beginning because as you start to add different rhythms, double up notes, and displace octaves you end up with endless possibilities. All derived off of one simple four note idea!

A jazz musician doesn't have enough hours in a day, enough days in a week, or enough years in a life to create, learn, and master all the new ideas that are possible. To understand what musicians see as a flow-thinker and what you see as a dam-thinker, go to a piano and try playing around. Try to improvise. Within a short period of time you will walk away. Why? Because you are unconstrained. You have no ideas. You don't see anything interesting you can do. You may even look at the piano and come to the conclusion that there isn't much you can do with it! If you own the piano you might want to sell it! That is exactly how many business leaders see their businesses today—uninteresting and virtually unusable. They may be so uninterested in the possibilities of their company that they just sell it. Yet, with only a few simple ideas, there is an almost infinite number of things you can do to improve your company!

Improvising is powerful—and it is extremely powerful when done within a team. Improvising completely blows open the learning dam. As your teams improvise, they learn to respect each other and all of the dams come down quickly like dominos crashing hard. Doing this will radically change your business. It takes time and effort to create a team that has mastered improvisation.

Figure 13: "Improvise" Spider Diagram

Improvising isn't taught in business schools these days, but it should be. The Toyota Production System was a complete improvisation. Toyota didn't have the equipment, the factory size, or the storage space, required for a U. S.-based automobile factory. These constraints produced a more efficient system. They took what they had and reorganized it in a different way, so that what they had would work. The result was something better and much more efficient than any other automobile manufacturer on the planet. Giving people more money, more equipment, and more workers will just produce more costs. When we receive what we ask for, unconstrained, we don't have the pressure to learn and discover something new. That is why it is important that a company set standards and constraints so that people can try different combinations of what they have and what they know, so that they can discover something new and better.

CHAPTER 10

Design Your Own Complex Plans

If you are out to describe the truth, leave elegance to the tailor.

—Albert Einstein

There I was, standing outside of the large glass doors to the large conference room at the Marriot Hotel in Minneapolis. I had rejoined my former company, AlliedSignal, after my departure from Monsanto. Standing there, looking through the glass doors, I knew I had blundered. Being over an hour late to an important meeting wasn't the type of mistake I wanted to make my first week on the job. However, it was in keeping with a tradition. As you will recall, the first time I was hired by AlliedSignal to work for this same business unit I was almost fired! Bob Floyd saved me, and I learned an important lesson about the power of listening and observing. I knew some of my friends would be very amused by my late arrival. I doubted that the energetic man speaking, Mark

Bulriss, the new president of AlliedSignal Laminate Systems, would appreciate or understand my mistake. I looked out over the room. It was a very large room with a very high, modern ceiling and a row of windows to the right, overlooking the roadway below.

Why was I late? Arizona is a state that doesn't change from standard time to daylight savings time. I didn't understand yet, since I recently moved to Arizona, that Arizona time would be two hours behind and sometimes one hour behind Central Standard Time. I had miscalculated the time change. I continued to look through the very large glass doors. The room was full with everyone sitting in very orderly, very neat rows. Everyone was sitting so stiffly. Nobody was gossiping or moving or whispering or making any kind of body movement. I had been to many large sales meetings before. I found them to be animated with plenty of movement, side conversations, and activity. I looked to the front of the room. I saw the pie charts and bar charts being presented by Mark. He was talking to a very large screen. He looked stern. He looked intense. And the slides I saw through the glass door looked like it was all detailed, internal financial stuff. I was perplexed. So I opened the door slowly. The floor was polished wood as if it were a basketball court. Everyone was so quiet that my footsteps reverberated loudly! Nobody looked back. Strange, I thought. Fortunately, Mark didn't stop talking, but he sure saw me walk in. I quickly took a seat in the back and listened.

As I listened, I was trying to understand what was driving this meeting. Why so much emphasis on financials? What was a *leaker list*? As I was to find out later, the leaker list was something Larry Bossidy, the CEO of AlliedSignal at the time, used to identify which business units weren't meeting his financial objectives. If you remained on the list, your company would be removed—sold. Larry held all of the leaders of Allied's businesses to a financial standard and made each of them accountable for their performance to that standard. If you didn't live up to the grade you would be vanquished from the company. Apparently, AlliedSignal Laminate Systems was coming very close to making the leaker list. Mark looked very concerned. I felt very concerned too. I felt that if we made the leaker list, we would all go down with the ship, never to be seen again, lifeless and dead. Mark's speech was creating a high degree of anxiety for me—and for everyone, for that matter.

But this was a sales meeting! How was talking about internal financial numbers going to help this company develop better customer relations that would lead to higher profits? How was it going to get the sales force motivated? I was wondering why there wasn't talk about customers? Who were the key customers? What were customers saying about our products and our services? What were the strategies we could use to get new products out and penetrate more market share? And then I saw it. The big blue corporate banner hanging from the rafters in the back just to the left of me. It looked like something that should be hanging in the Smithsonian. It was huge. You couldn't take your eyes off the huge AlliedSignal logo, printed in white. Below this logo were three statements that went something like this: 1. We will meet all of our financial commitments; 2. We will improve the costs of doing business through operational excellence; 3. We will make sure we meet all of our customer requirements. These were the directives that Larry Bossidy had delivered to every business unit leader. There was no discussion. There was no debate. If you didn't follow these three things you would be fired. And nothing was more important than the first item, delivering on financial commitments.

Larry had become CEO of AlliedSignal after working for Jack Welch at GE. Larry was the president of the very successful GE Capital, which had grown like a weed under his leadership. Jack, in his book, *Straight from the Gut,* explains in detail his respect for Larry Bossidy. Larry was not someone you let down. He was powerful. He was intimidating. But he was also extremely fair and honest. He was someone who, after talking to him, made you feel like you didn't want to let him down. Larry was a motivator in the best sense.

After the talk, Mark asked if there were any questions. There was a long silence. I broke the silence. I said, speaking very loudly because I was in the back, "Is that our banner?" There was dead silence. Mark got off the podium and started walking toward me. You could loudly hear each foot step as he approached. As he was walking toward me he replied, "No, it isn't; I am going to tell Larry Bossidy that we have a different banner!" I said, "Well, the banner is upside down." Mark quickly shut me down and made it clear that any further discussion just wouldn't be tolerated.

Some months later, Larry Bossidy had the executive presidents pull people together to find out, essentially, why customers had such a negative attitude about doing business with AlliedSignal. Under Larry's reign, AlliedSignal was gathering information all the time. Were people happy working for the company? Were we serving the right markets? Did customers like doing business with us? Larry didn't trust just looking at the financial data and information delivered by his IT department and his IT software packages. He needed more. He traveled all the time to plants and got to know many of the managers, as well as thousands of employees. But Larry didn't always trust his gut. He wanted to check and challenge his thinking. Not everyone understood this need that Larry had. If you, as a manger, started to blow a smoke screen, you would be cut down quickly. Larry wanted the truth. He knew something wasn't right with how AlliedSignal did business with customers, and he wanted to get to the bottom of it fast.

So, there was a very big meeting in Morristown, New Jersey—corporate headquarters. AlliedSignal Laminate Systems was part of AlliedSignal's chemical group, which was managed by its executive president, Fred Poses (Fred, a few years later, became the CEO of American Standard). Each of the three multibillion dollar divisions met with its lead executive. In Fred's meeting, it was noted that someone said that at a recent Laminate Systems sales meeting, the AlliedSignal banner was upside down. I was told that Fred's initial reply was, "Larry would never go for putting financials last!" Fred apparently did bring this up to Larry, because the banner was changed to something like, 1. We will always strive to exceed our customer's needs and expectations; 2. We will improve using operational excellence; 3. We will meet our financial commitments. Even though the banner was turned upside down, the financials were still in the forefront of everyone's mind. Customer relations did improve, but not dramatically.

At the time of the sales meeting in Minneapolis, I came to learn that Mark was under a great deal of pressure. Before his arrival, Laminate Systems was decaying. Mark knew customers were important, but he also knew he had to conform to what Larry Bossidy needed, and he needed financial results and profits fast. Even though Mark was a little hard on me in that first sales meeting, he enthusiastically supported me through the registration work at Continental (later to become Sanmina, Phoenix) and paid attention to my phone calls, emails, and suggestions for him to improve. Mark was clearly a very tolerant and patient man underneath it all. Based on one of my recommendations, he got himself a copy of the book *Chaos,* by James Gleick, and read it. When we were at Morristown, and after Larry had talked to our small group in the meet and greet (our small group was going to be presented with the Premier Achievement Award for Customer

Satisfaction), Mark said I was the butterfly that flapped its wings that day in the sales meeting. The *butterfly effect* describes what is possible in a complex system such as weather: a butterfly flapping its wings in China could create a hurricane in the Bahamas. Within a complex system, anyone can have an unpredictable and unexpectedly large impact, but nobody has more potential impact on a complex system then the leader of the business—the CEO.

After Mark left (eventually to become CEO of Great Lakes Chemical) Larry Bossidy eventually hired Steve Hochhauser as the new president of Laminate Systems. Steve understood Laminate Systems' business, as well as its competitors, because he was president of another division that supplied electro-deposited copper foil to laminate systems. This foil is essential to printed circuit board laminate. Steve understood a great problem Laminate Systems had. It is a problem that plagues many companies today, and that is accountability. Steve was a stocky man. He was originally from Brooklyn, New York. He was scrappy. He loved to talk. He was enthusiastic and very social. He wore his feelings on his sleeve. And he would tell you exactly what he was thinking—unfiltered. He would give me a hard, enthusiastic handshake whenever we met.

Steve had a talent for instantly seeing a situation and what needed to be done to get people moving. He understood people. He had a way of communicating that was disarming and intense at the same time. Part of his charm was that he was always informal. Steve spent endless hours, days, weeks, and months talking to people in a very social and passionate way. After listening to what you had to say, or him relaying a story to you, he would look into your eyes and say very passionately and sincerely, "You, as an employee of this company, must make good on your commitments. I must make good on my commitments to you, to myself, to our customers, and to this company. I expect the same from you in return. We must never fail in the commitments we make to our customers." And then he would add, "We are all going to be part of a great company here. I want to hear how you think this company can be great." Under Steve's leadership, the culture at AlliedSignal Laminate Systems (that was improving under Mark Bulris) improved very rapidly. Eventually, Laminate Systems was sold just after the merger of AlliedSignal and Honeywell. The new company became Isola Laminate Systems and is very successful today. After the acquisition, Steve left to join Johns Manville, where he eventually became CEO, reporting to Warren Buffet.

THE DIFFERENCE BETWEEN COMPLEX AND COMPLICATED

Complicated and complex are two very different things. Many business leaders make things too complicated. They try to do too many things. They take too many steps. And they do entirely too much planning when they should just be doing. Complicated often means different ways of doing the same thing over and over again—much like the fly, hitting up against the window, in the book *You²* by Price Pritchett. The fly tries again and again through raw determination to go through the glass window. It is unaware that, a few feet away, there is an open door. Not seeing the open door, the fly eventually fails and dies. Hitting the glass again and again in business most often manifests itself by adding more rules, more management, more procedures, more data collection, more forms, more reports, and more oversight. This all adds up to more non-value-added work that creates more solid dams that stop all flows. And it is all a result of an inability to change how we think. We like to stick to our existing dam paradigms even if the open door to what we seek just requires a slight turn of the head to see.

I remember when I was in Morristown, yet again for a training program, this time as a product development master (PDM). Larry Bossidy came walking in with his trench coat and spoke to all of us. It was a cold, cloudy day, with old ice and snow on the ground. There was nothing to think about other than work. This was my third encounter with him in less than two years. I was a worker bee, but very valuable. I make this point to show just how far Larry's reach was. He explained that AlliedSignal couldn't rely on just taking cost out of operations and doing Six Sigma. The company needed to be more creative. Fred Poses, the night before, also gave us a talk; he said that every employee needed to be more creative. A creative mantra had been started, but did it have legs? Nobody seemed to know how to drive creativity. The idea behind the PDMs was that creativity could be improved in the same way that costs were removed using Six Sigma. This proved, unsurprisingly, not to work—at all!

I had spent a few days of very complicated training prior to Larry walking into our session. I was sitting at a desk, almost as if I were in school, with my name displayed prominently on a piece of cardboard in front of me. I couldn't help myself. I asked Larry how he was going to help us become more creative. There was a pause. He walked over in my direction and took a good look at my name. Eventually, he smiled and told our group that he would support us in anything we came up with. To be fair, at that time I sure didn't know what the right answer was to improve creativity. I was very ignorant about the nature, dynamics and chaos of a creative system.

Prior to my question, Larry said that he wanted people talking more in the lunchroom area, putting ideas up on the wall randomly, and thinking freely. What he said sounded so easy that it appeared trivial at first glance, but it was absolutely the right answer—a powerful answer. What Larry said was different. It wasn't his usual message at all. It suggested a different way to work together. It was about being spontaneous, improvisational, and uncertain. It was about an environment where new ideas would emerge. This was exactly the opposite approach of what we were learning within an almost assembly-line process that demanded certainty. A creative process that was a derivative of Six Sigma didn't have any chance at all to be successful. Creativity isn't predictable. You can't force it like an assembly line.

Larry somehow knew this, but at the time he may not have fully appreciated the value of his suggestion. Working together socially in the lunchroom and playing around with random ideas was what Pixar did. In order for such a thing to work at AlliedSignal, all dams would have to come down and the company would have to convert to a flow paradigm. It would mean a whole different way of organizing jobs, work, and people. It would probably demand a different architecture for all of the buildings— at the very least, widely different floor plans that would change the way people were organized. For example, after Pixar made a lot of money, they designed their new headquarters specifically for complex social interactions that would be amplified. Larry just didn't have enough time to make AlliedSignal maximally creative. And there were very few people at that time who really understood how to make an organization creative. Very soon, after my PDM training, Larry decided to merge with Honeywell.

When a company runs out of growth space, it looks for a different way to grow, and one way is through mergers and acquisitions. Green Giant with Pillsbury; Pillsbury with Grand Met; AOL with Time Warner; Monsanto with G. D. Searle; Shipley with Rohm and Haas; and AlliedSignal with Honeywell. Few leaders realize the true importance of their name. For example, Shipley was a powerful name in the production of printed circuit boards and semiconductor chips. It carried with it a high level of respect within the entire electronics industry. Yet Rohm and Haas decided to drop the name completely. This caused everyone to wonder about the product. If the name was changed, what else was changed? After all, a name and what it stands for is abstract, not real. But what people identify in a name is more real than any product or service or action. Names are complex. Change it and it causes a whole bunch of other stuff to happen. When you kill the name, you kill the identity, you wash away the culture, you dilute what made the company great. When you change the name, you blow up the brand. The brand is a complex pattern in our brain that makes our buying decisions easy. When the brand is gone we feel adrift, lost, and insecure, because we have to go out and find a new brand that we can trust and can rely on. The name change itself is one of many reasons why few great companies become better through a merger or acquisition. The reason why a business name is so important, the reason why a creative workspace and environment is so important, the reason why a single idea conveyed socially by a CEO is so important, is because all of these things amplify positive results within a complex business system. All business systems are complex because all businesses consist of people and their social networks.

Nothing is more complex than a relationship between a man and a woman. One of the better books that can help you understand this complexity is *Men are Easy* by Lynn Rasmussen. The traditional way many experts like to talk about marriage is in terms of compromise: the man and woman must learn to compromise. Right? Rasmussen's view is simple, "Why compromise?" She goes on to explain that couples should focus on designing the life they want together and compromise nothing. Shoot for the best! Aim for the stars! What she says is completely perpendicular to the common view: the *compromise* paradigm. For example, in a relationship that operates under a *compromise* paradigm, we cling to certainty and avoid uncertainty. She says, though, that in a relationship operating under a *design* paradigm we should step out of certainty and entertain uncertainty! In this book, the *certainty* paradigm would imply dams (ego, trust, feelings, My Precious, and learning) and a lack of flow, producing pressure, pollution, and stagnation. As a result, the probability of a relationship surviving isn't very high. Could this way of thinking—compromise—actually be the source of so many failed marriages?

With a *design* paradigm that entertains and expects uncertainty, the couple can be much more experimental, much more collaborative, much more open to learning new things, much more humble, and much more supportive. Just changing the expectation from holding fast to certainty to creating and welcoming uncertainty changes the way people think, changes the way people interact with one another, and changes the probability of a successful marriage. When we entertain uncertainty, we expect the unexpected. We expect emergence. Few business leaders welcome uncertainty and fewer still trust emergence, especially when they have no control over it or the ability to predict it! Yet that is absolutely required if your company is to become creative and realize unlimited growth. You must entertain uncertainty. You must allow you and your people to shoot for the stars. You must not tolerate compromise. Why would you?

The modern understanding of complexity really comes from chaos theory. Contained within chaos theory are very advanced ideas of scale. For example, the advanced animations found in movies and videogames, with realistic landscapes and people, could not have been made without the advanced chaos idea called a fractal. A fractal is just a simple rule, which exploits an iterative and flowing concept of scale. To understand fractals, draw an equilateral triangle. Then draw on the middle third of each face another equilateral triangle. Repeat this process over and over again and you get a very complex looking surface created from a very simple equation. That is exactly the type of program that is used to create realistic-looking animations. This exactly explains a key component of a complex system: a very simple rule repeated in a feedback loop. Steve Hochhauser used a simple rule by stating that everyone needed to live up to their commitments, and he tirelessly created feedback around that idea. This caused the AlliedSignal Laminate systems culture to change rapidly.

There is another key scale feature to fractals and complex systems: fractals have self-similarity. What that means, as you zoom in, you see the same fractal image repeat itself again and again. It is as if scale has disappeared entirely. The pattern looks the same large as it does small. For example, stock prices have similar patterns over the course of a year as they do over the course of a day. If you were shown the two graphs separately without a time axis, it would be impossible to tell if the chart represented a year or a day.

This fractal idea and its self similarity provides a context for you to think about. For example, when Steve Hochhauser spent time and energy repeatedly pulling people aside and talking to them, he put something very complex into motion. Others in the company started to repeat what Steve was doing. The communication and idea and thinking started to merge, divide, and grow in a way similar to fractals. How people made good on their commitments, how they helped each other, how they held themselves and each other accountable became very social, very adaptable, and very complex. If you were blindfolded you couldn't tell if the conversation you heard was between workers or executives. The tone, the urgency, the words, the patterns would be indistinguishable. The type of culture change Steve created is almost impossible to understand in detail, because so many things happened all at once. That is why complex systems, by their nature, are massively parallel.

Another key concept to understand is that a complex system is like a spider web. A web, where when you change one thing it changes everything else. If you do things to produce a My Precious dam you will get the trust dam too. If you do things to remove the ego dam you will remove the learning dam too. There are many webs in an organization. You need to find the webs and find some of the connections. It is the connections that allow you to develop indirect complex solutions. It is why listening and observing builds trust. It is the same strategy that builds trust with Gorillas in the wild. Telling a Gorilla to trust you just wont work. What happens when all the thinking dams come down? You have a new web connecting communication, discovery, productivity, territory, and purpose. As you make these positive webs stronger you make the positive social webs connecting your people stronger. When this happens you have something truly wonderful, because as a single individual gets better everyone else gets better too. It is all nonlinear. It is all dynamic. It is all uncertain. When you know how to manage a complex system it is all good.

Businesses, by the fact they are complex social networks connecting people, will always be complex, no matter how hard you try to enforce your departmentalized organization chart. When you ignore complexity, complexity will work against you.

IDEAS ON HOW TO DESIGN A BUSINESS
THAT FLOWS & GROWS

Start with an ambitious goal. What do you and your company want to become? Use your wildest dream and fantasy. Hold nothing back. Release yourself of all mental baggage. In Lynn Rasmussen's book, *Men are Easy*, she says, "Dream up an ideal situation. Think 'pie in the sky.' Imagine how you want the outcome to look and feel." As a business leader you shouldn't compromise either. You need to set a fantastic goal for you and your company. And then you need to visualize what it will be like when it manifests itself into reality.

When you make the explicit decision to go after the *pie-in-the-sky* goal and make it a reality, you will move yourself and the web you are connected to, everything connected to your life, everything connected to your company, up. You will force people that believe in your vision to change for the better, and force the others that don't believe in your vision to leave. Think back to the decisions the criminals had to make in New York City when mayor Giuliani enforced actions consistent with the theory of no *broken windows*: the criminals had to change their life or leave the city!

When you dedicate your company to the fantastic goal, you haven't just changed a rule or changed the workplace environment, rather, with a single stroke you have changed the entire reason for the existence of your business. You did what the late Ward Cosgrove did way back when Green Giant was the humble Minnesota Valley Canning Company. You did what Earl Bakken did when Medtronic was just a company of very few employees and he dreamed up an inconceivable 100-year plan. You did what my grandfather did when created his small venture capital company called Community Investment Enterprises, which helped many young entrepreneurs become incredibly successful. Nothing is more powerful and beneficial for you than creating and then committing to a pie-in-the-sky goal.

No function in any company is more important than human resources and yet, in many companies, it is the most undervalued asset. Consider Robert I. Sutton's book, *The No Asshole Rule.* In it, Sutton talks about a consulting firm that clearly operates within a flow paradigm. The company name is IDEO. You may not have heard of them. Go to their website. You will immediately discover that they are very different. They are extremely provocative. Sutton says, "IDEO is one of the most successful innovation firms in the world." And in order to do that they "aggressively screen out demeaning and arrogant people." IDEO understands explicitly that work is social. Without human beings interacting and collaborating, they would not be innovative. They wouldn't be productive. But they also take things an important step farther. As Sutton says, "Every candidate is interviewed by people who will be above, below, and alongside them, status-wise. And people from unrelated professional disciplines participate." Why? As Sutton describes, individual managers tend to hire clones of themselves, which means if you hire an asshole you can expect in time you will have exponentially more assholes. IDEO's rule of having very different people involved in the hiring process prevents this from happening. The No Asshole Rule is a single, simple rule that can produce a powerful result.

I have discussed at length the importance of designing the workspace environment, which includes a small number of simple rules about how people need to work together. If you decide to move your company in this direction, you need to make sure you let your work teams participate in the transformation. Let the team design the workspaces based on your guidelines. If you remember, Miles, in his *Kind of Blue* recording session, walked in with just a few simple chords. He let the rest of the group fill in all of the details, and when he had to play his solo, he had to fit in all of the decisions the others had already made! And he made all of this happen in real time!

With your guidance, let the team determine the work to be done and who does the work. Have the team commit to the timing and the results through a negotiation with you and the customer. Have the team manage and be accountable for the results. When the project is done, allow the team to break up and join other teams. What I am describing is similar to how Pixar operates. Moreover, this type of work environment is the basis of Ken Schwaber's and Jeff Sutherland's ideas about SCRUM. As a leader of a business system that flows and grows, you must trust the surprising and chaotic ways things emerge. Setting up your operation this way will attract highly talented and creative people, especially when it is combined with your pie-in-the-sky goal.

What about the information and reports you think you need in order to run the business? In a dam-thinking company, collection of information is meant to validate people's beliefs and is not meant to create discovery, learning, or change people's thinking. In a dam-thinking company, it is not meant to generate new ideas, new directions, or new growth. Hence, IT efforts in dam-thinking companies are wasteful and generate little value. In a business that has been scaled very large, people attempt to gather hoards of information and then they attempt to make sense of it. All of this becomes very expensive. All of this requires exponential increases in capital and resources. Oracle, SAP, SAS, IBM, and Microsoft make tremendous amounts of money trying to help businesses collect vast streams of information and analyze this information using their software. As your information systems grow in size and become more complicated, delays increase and the likelihood of implementation issues grows exponentially. You have pressure, pollution, and stagnation—the hallmarks of dam-thinking.

There are two serious problems with these systems. First, you have to conform to the information system because the information system itself has limited flexibility and adaptability. Second, as the information system grows in size and scope, it starts to prohibit people from making real observations about your company's work and what is really happening. If you are not careful, you will start to believe the reports are reality and what is really going on with your people is a fiction. When that happens, disaster is just around the corner.

What is the alternative? Your lawyer, your doctor, your stock broker, and your IT software company would like you to believe that you don't know enough to make an informed decision. They want you to relinquish control because they are the experts! But nobody cares more about your money, your health, your legal risks, and your company than you do. You should never delegate the thinking, the understanding, and the decision making to others. Because you are a flow-thinker, you can change the relationship with your IT supplier. Demand that their system conform to and add value to your flow system. In order to do that, the software system must be appropriately scaled to your business system. Any implementation must be scaled in such a way as to encourage maximum success, and not scaled so large that it guarantees failure. Always ask for the minimal system. Set a very short timeline for the implementations. Set the standard that the system must be simple and adaptable.

You might consider the idea of having a real-time information system with no computers and software to start. Use the model my grandfather implemented with the schoolteachers observing the Green Giant canning operations (described in Chapter 2). My father used to say, "Why do you want, artificial intelligence when you can have real intelligence?" Have motivated, intelligent people, perhaps college students in search of a project, or fresh college graduates that want a job but don't have the experience, collect information, analyze the information in real time, and produce simple, powerful reports so that you can see how your business is really doing. Think about all of the observational information that you would have at your fingertips and how much deeper you would understand the numbers and see the patterns. Imagine how much better you would be able to design your own information system working with SAP, Oracle, IBM, or SAS.

You might challenge your IT supplier further. For any significant IT purchase, you should ask the supplier if they use their own software. The next question is to have them show you how they use the software and how that has benefited them. And the last question should be why they use the software the way they do and not another way.

STORY POINT 11:
Develop A Simple Complex Plan That Deals
With Immediate Reality

In Chapter 9, we learned that you need very few ideas to create a vast array of approaches that can create surprising and good results. The same is true for your complex plan. You only need a few ideas. Start in any order you want. Before you know it, you will have a very dynamic and profitable company on your hands. The next figure shows the ideas already introduced from the previous story points. I show the walls of the dam disappearing on the left. Think of this as the current state of a dam-thinking culture. The various complex solutions are shown parallel to each other on the right and the far right are the results you can expect when you have achieved in your future state: your flow-thinking culture. The parallel depiction emphasizes the parallel nature of your complex plan. You will be doing many things at once in parallel. You will see many different results emerge in parallel. With each complex solution comes an improvement in a flow, and it, too, emerges in parallel. Complex plans, by design, are massively parallel!

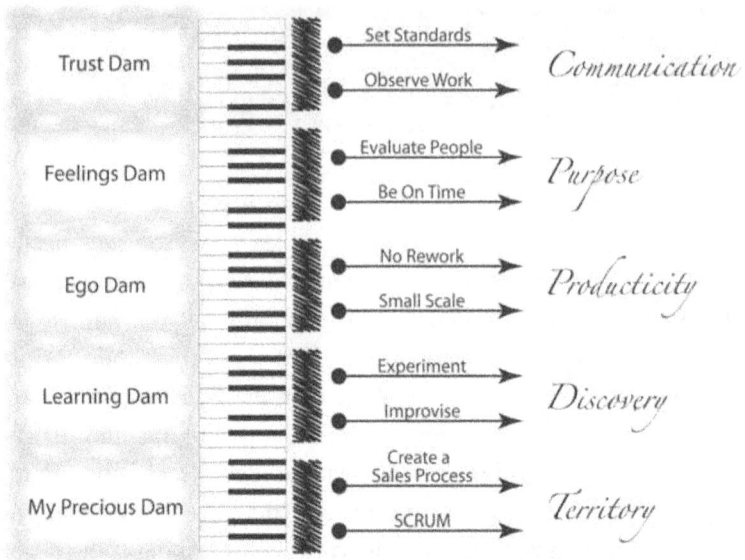

Trust Dam	Set Standards → / Observe Work →	*Communication*
Feelings Dam	Evaluate People → / Be On Time →	*Purpose*
Ego Dam	No Rework → / Small Scale →	*Producticity*
Learning Dam	Experiment → / Improvise →	*Discovery*
My Precious Dam	Create a Sales Process → / SCRUM →	*Territory*

Figure 14: Designing The Plan

The figure above depicts how you should think about designing your complex plan. You have the problems on the left, the thinking dams, which I show dissolving. This illustrates your current state. You have the desired outcomes on the right, which illustrate your future state. In the middle, I show how you can go from the current state to the future state. You have individual solutions to each dam, which come from the previous story points. You have the keyboard that symbolizes the nonlinear way you can order and play your plan. There is no right or wrong. There is no perfect plan. There is just doing. Everything is in parallel in this figure because a complex plan generates massively parallel activities and outcomes.

Where should you start? Your complex plan doesn't have to have a lot of detail. The emphasis should be on doing. As things emerge, you observe, learn, adapt again in a simple way, always moving forward. Think of it like a game of chess. Let me give you an easy example of how to get started with this. A friend of mine, Bill Sezate, was concerned about his son's grades in his calculus 3 class; in fact, he was teetering on failure. Bill's son's name was Grahm. Grahm was very smart. He had gotten a car, a job, and a girlfriend. Bill thought Grahm wasn't doing his homework. How would you approach this problem and what would be your plan? That is, what would be your linear dam-thinking plan? What would be your complex flow-thinking plan? What type of plan would add to the father-son relationship more?

Bill took Grahm out to dinner to listen to his story, where he learned that a number of his assumptions about his son's bad grades were wrong. Grahm was doing all of his homework, but the teacher didn't give any credit for the homework, nor would the teacher tutor the students so that they could complete the homework more easily thereby gaining a command of the material. Grahm, in the past, relied on this review of the homework with the teacher. Bill said, "Son, why don't we get you a tutor?"

Grahm rejected this because he felt he didn't need one and shouldn't have to have one—and there was a social stigma at school for having a tutor. Bill talked to me about his son's problem. It was clear that his son had an ego dam that was getting in the way of his productive growth. We turned to the figure above and looked at the two recommended complex solutions for an ego dam: *no rework* and *small scale.*

How were these solutions translated and applied in order to come up with a powerful complex plan? The no rework complex solution could be understood, in this case, as not repeating a class. The small scale complex solution could be understood as increasing the focus (temporarily) on the challenge before the son: how to overcome the difficult teacher. So instead of saying, "You have to keep all of your grades high," he was going to focus on, "How are you going to overcome this specific problem?" Bill also decided to add another complex solution element. He decided to make Grahm responsible for developing his own solution. In this case, the father was letting go of his own My Precious dam and expanding his son's territory and responsibility.

The plan was put in motion. Bill said to Grahm that he could no longer see his girlfriend or have access to the car. This was not meant as punishment, but was meant to provide an environment in which he could concentrate on the problem at hand. The problem was how to overcome the teacher who refused to tutor him in the way Grahm had grown accustomed to. Bill said to Grahm, "Your life will be full of roadblocks. If you learn how to overcome this roadblock and find your own solution, you will discover many things about yourself and many things about the nature of complex-problem solving that will propel you to a very successful and fulfilling life." Grahm passed the class, but it wasn't his usual A. What Grahm learned was more valuable than the A and that was how to create and apply a complex plan.

Do complex plans really work? Let's return to Gerstner's book, *Who Says Elephants Can't Dance?*. Chapter 22 of this book talks about the eight leading principles Gerstner launched almost all at once—more or less pushing all the keys on the keyboard down—in order to change the culture of IBM fast. He hatched a massively parallel complex plan. His first principle, *the marketplace is the driving force behind everything we do at IBM,* shows us a new complex solution that we could use within our own complex planning activities: focus on the marketplace and serve your customers instead of an internal notion of what customers want. This pulls at an ego dam (ask customers for help) and a learning dam (learn what the customer wants). He goes on with seven more principles, all of which pull on thinking dams, and all of which represent complex solutions you can try.

EPILOGUE

You Will Attract What You Think

If you think you can, you can.
And if you think you can't, you're right.

—Mary Kay Ash

It was a beautiful sunset in front of me as I climbed out of the Mississippi river valley, up a bluff face well over 500 feet in elevation, with Lacrosse, Wisconsin, behind me on my way to Rochester, Minnesota, to attend my Dale Carnegie class. I was a young man working for my third company, still driving my first car, a Chevy S10 Blazer, and it was late March 1986. My car radio had a cassette player and I was listening to one of those motivational speaking tapes. I had to make this long drive because of my bad behavior that first week on the job working for Bob Floyd. He sent me to Dale Carnegie School. Because my case was an emergency, Bob didn't want me to wait for the next class in Lacrosse. The drive from Lacrosse to Rochester was a 60-minute drive, one way! And I did it, back and forth over 12 trips, one trip every week. I would leave work at 4:50 PM in order to be at class before 6:00 PM, which ended at 9:30 PM, and I would be home close to 11:00 PM.

To keep me awake, I ordered a bunch of self-improvement tapes from a company called Nightingale-Conant, as well as other similar companies. I really enjoyed these tapes. I discovered Zig Zigler and Dr. Wayne Dyer. All of these people left an impression on me. They resonated with me because they echoed what had been told to me by a single mother some nine years prior when I was a discouraged 20-year-old man.

As a young man, I had allowed negative thoughts to permeate my head. My dad, who was a brilliant surgeon, was never happy with my scholastic performance. He used to give me his Gentleman's C lecture, starting at about the time I was in junior high. He started out by drawing a bell-shaped curve and lopping off the top 5 percent. This 5 percent, the people who made the top grades, were the people I wanted to be with; otherwise I would have a bad life. This lecture produced worry for me and made me feel like my life was doomed. My dad saw an absolute one-to-one correlation between how well you did in school and how well you did in life. After drawing the curve, he would say I was destined to have that Gentleman's C, which was bad, because without an A grade-point average, I would never own a Mercedes, I would not live in a nice house, I would never have a good job, and I certainly would never have a significant patent, write numerous articles, travel the world, speak to hundreds of people, or have my own business, let alone write a book. I didn't know at the time that my dad's theory was dead wrong. And by listening to him, I had allowed my subconscious to imprint a Gentleman's C and the bell-shaped curve—the world of limits—onto my brain.

People learn and experience the world and grow in different ways. The educational system today has failed to recognize this and adapt to it, and I feel this can be damaging to young people who don't excel scholastically, but have very great talent and aptitude. My Meyer's–Brigg's Personality Test is INTP. That means I am introverted, intuitive, thinking, and perceptive; I like to think long and hard and really understand a subject. This takes time, and education today is impatient and doesn't like to wait for answers. A well-thought-out answer that might take months, sometimes years to emerge, isn't a skill taught in today's education system. Einstein was an INTP and so were Newton and Eisenhower. Einstein and Eisenhower did really poorly in school. Did you know that Ansel Adams, the great photographer, could not function in a normal school classroom and was patiently home schooled by his father? Ansel stood no chance for success within a traditional school system. Is it any wonder that some notable people seem to start businesses without completing their education or taking the education system seriously. Bill Gates and Steve Jobs did not place a primary importance on grades because their focus was on a dream. Gates liked to play poker, and his poker mates became his business partners. Jobs liked to hang out at Atari with his friend Steve Wozniak creating, at times, black market, borderline-illegal electronic stuff. Even with this strong evidence, the harmful myth of grades and success and the bell curve philosophy continues to spread like weeds. A typical academic counselor might try to tell kids to accept less in life, strictly based on grades and standardized test scores. This kills dreams. This kills futures. And it often rewards the wrong dam-thinking behaviors.

Do we want to teach our kids that they live in a world of limited possibility or that they live in a world of infinite abundance. Which paradigm attracts kids to drugs? I love education. I do not love the education system. The education system found in most primary and secondary schools fails to teach students how to learn. It fails to teach students how to deal with complex problems. It fails to teach students how to be maximally effective by working with others. Improvisation, parallel thinking, and mastermind techniques just aren't on the curriculum and yet these techniques are the gateway of unlimited possibilities.

It was a system that made me a discouraged young man during my summers in college, in which I worked in the surgical lab at the Minneapolis Veteran's Administration hospital. I got to know many of the good people who worked there. One was a single mom who had raised—on her own—her son who was in high school. Her son ran cross country and track, and she got him a job in the lab. He and I started running together, and I started to take him under my wing, functioning as sort of a big brother. Seeing how I was encouraging her son, the mom decided to return the favor in order to encourage and help me. She saw my discouragement and worry. She basically told me, "All of us have something we want inside us in order to feel fulfilled. If we don't know what that is, then we need to work hard to figure out what it is. When we find it, then we need to have the courage to think about it and believe in ourselves. When we do that, we will be guided to it, and it will become reality. I absolutely believe in this." When she finished, she didn't say anything more about it nor did she ever bring it up again. I had never heard anything like this. It went against my programming, but I couldn't let what she said go. She planted a seed and I could not stop thinking about it.

After that conversation, I started to ignore and then reject the bell-shaped curve philosophy that outlined a limited possibility space where only the supremely gifted were entitled. I decided, before graduating from St. Olaf College, that I would go to the University of Minnesota to become a chemical engineer. I had decided I wanted that, and I was going to become that, and there just was no stopping me. When the university wanted to reject my application because of a grade point average that was a perfect Gentleman's C, but included crazy courses such as abstract algebra, advanced organic chemistry, and music theory II (without taking music theory I) I drove over to the dean of admissions office and told him why I belonged in the chemical engineering program and that I would be in the program—period. Saying no to me was not one of his options. He seemed very frustrated. I countered all of his concerns. Finally, he grew sick of the debate. He made a deal with me, which he thought would end in failure for me, and which I saw as a perfect opportunity, the crack in the door I needed. He told me to go over to Amundson Hall and find a professor who would sponsor me to let me in the school. If I could find someone willing to do that, then they would have to select a course for me to take during the summer—and if I didn't get an A, I wouldn't be accepted, and he would make sure I never visited his office again.

Not to be deterred, and completely focused on what I wanted, I marched out of his office with my transcripts and summer catalogue in hand and headed toward Amundson Hall. Office after office was vacant. Very few professors were still on campus because they were between the end of the spring semester and the beginning of the summer session. By the time I reached the third floor, I poked my head into an office that was piled high with books; journals and papers were everywhere. There was an open window with a small fan blowing air over the desk of Herbert Isbin, one of the pioneers in advanced nuclear reactors. His daughter, Sharon Isbin, grew up to become one of the best classical guitarists in the world. He looked at me, surprised, and his eyes told me he was thinking, "What are you doing here?" He didn't say a word. I walked in and sat down. I started to explain my story. As I was talking, he motioned for the transcripts and the catalogue. He studied the transcripts carefully. He had turned to the side, with one ear listening and his eyes slowly looking at the transcript line by line by line. To this day, I think he saw something in it he recognized: a personality type, someone he knew, or a student he used to have. As I was still talking, he turned, put down the transcripts and picked up the catalogue. His face disappeared from me as he held it closely to his face; he flipped through it. As I was still talking, he dropped the catalogue revealing his face, a face that was painted with a warm smile. He took a pen and circled a class. He said, "Take this one." And then said, "Tell the dean that Professor Herbert Isbin will be your sponsor." I walked out. The course that Mr. Isbin selected for me was inorganic chemistry. I already saw the A in my mind. And I got an A. I got into the school, and I became a very successful chemical engineer.

How did this happen, going from a Gentleman's C to getting an A in a challenging class without breaking a sweat? I always had the aptitude and the talent to get A's. My IQ is very high. But the thought of that Gentleman's C in my head had dammed up my performance. I had allowed my ego to accept my fate without question! I did not want to bother asking how to go higher! Ego can make you think you are better than you truly are or worse than you truly are. Few people understand that. Many feel you are better without an ego and it's bad when you have an ego. That is nonsense. We all have an ego. We need one. We just have to learn to manage it and not have it get in the way of us living our lives to the fullest.

The subconscious mind can't filter or reject a thought or idea coming from our conscious mind, such as a Gentleman's C. For example, by listening to my father, and listening to his bell-shaped curve philosophy, and listening to the Gentleman's C lecture, and accepting it into my day-to-day thinking, I had imprinted a lot of negative ideas into my subconscious mind. And as a result, that is exactly what I got. It didn't matter if it was an easy class or an impossible class, I would get a C. I am sure Isbin saw this when he closely studied my transcripts.

If I had been thinking A's and A's only, I would likely have gotten A's. When I thought only about getting into the chemical engineering program and getting an A, with no doubts in my head and a total belief that I would accomplish it, I got what I had worked so hard for—finally. A great gift had been given me. I would not have developed as a person if the dean of admissions had simply let me into the school. This one event changed the course of my life.

You still may not believe in the power of thought and mind, image and visualization, the subconscious mind and the conscious mind, so let me continue with my story. In the car, driving to my Dale Carnegie class, I started to think about what I wanted, what I liked, what I would like to do, what interested me, and what my perfect life might look like. One of those things was having my own consulting business one day. I had other thoughts too. I thought about how much I admired Frank Lloyd Wright and his Taliesin West buildings. I spent countless hours staring at pictures of the structure, trying to understand it from the time I was a little kid. He and his buildings, especially Taliesin West, fascinated me. I wanted a home that had big glass windows, with nothing but nature behind me. I thought about being financially independent. I thought about riding my bike through the hills of Tuscany. I thought about writing many articles and making significant advancements in the industry I worked in. I allowed all of it to float around in my mind unfiltered—just imagining—as I watched the miles tick away on that long straight road driving down I-90.

Over the next 5, 15, and 20 years, I solved the multilayer printed circuit registration problem and developed a patent for AlliedSignal. I authored many articles. I moved to Scottsdale, Arizona, living within two miles of Taliesin West, in a house composed of glass walls and a backyard right behind a nature preserve. I became financially independent. And I did take that bike trip with Butterfield & Robinson through the hills of Tuscany. You attract to yourself what you think—both positive and negative. Control your mind; control your life!

When I had all but given up on my consulting business, I met a business man in Las Vegas. He said, "Are you just going to remain content or are you going to figure out what you want and go get it," and he said this within one minute of our first handshake. Within a month, I figured out what my ideal client looked like: high technology, small, and wanting to grow, learn, and be different, but in trouble. Within six months I had an ideal client—a client that generated huge professional growth for me. My consulting business was finally launched for real.

A few years later I crossed paths with that business man again. As if reading my mind he said, "You should write a book. I know what it would be about. I can see it in my mind. And I know exactly how you should sign it. Gray, you will write this book. You have no idea what it will do for your business and for your life." And so I wrote this book. A book I had been thinking about for a very long time. You attract to you what you want. The human mind is a very powerful instrument.

My dad had an extremely gifted and strong mind. I remember the hours he would spend reading medical journals in his home office. Besides being a brilliant thoracic surgeon, he pioneered head and neck surgery. He spent thousands of hours studying and thinking about esophageal cancer. He desperately wanted to figure out a treatment that would provide hope to people for one of the deadliest of all cancers, but he just couldn't find a way. At the age of 76, he was diagnosed with esophageal cancer and died within a few months. My dad never encouraged me to go into medicine, and I am forever grateful for that in many ways.

You may still not believe me, but think back on the turning points in your life—both good and bad—and try to remember what you were thinking about. Write it all out and see if you see a pattern. This is important for you to do because your company will flow and grow only if you see it happening. With that, you will have the motivation to remove the thinking dams very quickly, and you will remove them. By placing the right ideas in your head and with your employees in line with those ideas (as a mission that they see happening too) your company will experience unlimited growth. Only then will you attract to you what your company needs to flow and grow. The first task assigned to Earl Bakken by my grandfather was to craft a mission statement that he and his company could believe in and dedicate themselves to. This was the story that Earl shared at my grandfather's memorial service.

In the end, it is never just about business. It is about the quality of the life you choose for yourself and the positive energy you apply to make it happen.

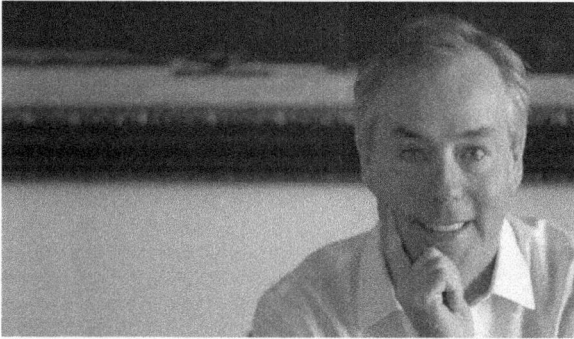

ABOUT GRAY MCQUARRIE

Gray McQuarrie is founder and president of Grayrock & Associates, LLC and founder of the Flow Thinkers Group.

Gray is the primary inventor for the patent Compensation Model and Registration Simulation Apparatus and Method for Manufacturing Printed Circuit Boards which increased productivity between suppliers and fabricators in this global industry on an exponential scale. He has worked for and consulted with small companies as well as Fortune 100 companies. A six sigma black belt, a product development master, and winner of the premier achievement award for customer satisfaction given out by Larry Bossidy, CEO of AlliedSignal, Gray is passionate about developing systems that can be implemented quickly. He has a liberal arts education from St. Olaf College where he received a BA and a professional education from the University of Minnesota where he earned a degree in Chemical Engineering.

Gray is one of the few consultants who has to practice what he preaches everyday and this book is a reflection of that practical step-by-step approach to solving some of today's toughest business issues.

You can learn more about Gray and Grayrock & Associates, LLC at www.grayrock.net.

www.ingramcontent.com/pod-product-compliance
Lightning Source LLC
Chambersburg PA
CBHW031925190326
41519CB00007B/420